THE CHILD'S REALITY:
Three Developmental Themes

JOHN M. MacEACHRAN MEMORIAL
LECTURE SERIES

Sponsored by
The Department of Psychology
The University of Alberta
with the support of
The Alma Mater Fund of the University of Alberta
in memory of John M. MacEachran,
pioneer in Canadian psychology

THE CHILD'S REALITY: Three Developmental Themes

David Elkind
University of Rochester

 LAWRENCE ERLBAUM ASSOCIATES, PUBLISHERS
1978   Hillsdale, New Jersey

DISTRIBUTED BY THE HALSTED PRESS DIVISION OF
JOHN WILEY & SONS
New York   Toronto   London   Sydney

Copyright© 1978 by Lawrence Erlbaum Associates, Inc.
   All rights reserved. No part of this book may be reproduced in
   any form, by photostat, microform, retrieval system, or any other
   means, without the prior written permission of the publisher.

Lawrence Erlbaum Associates, Inc., Publishers
62 Maria Drive
Hillsdale, New Jersey 07642

Distributed solely by Halsted Press Division
John Wiley & Sons, Inc., New York

Library of Congress Cataloging in Publication Data

Elkind, David, 1931–
   The child's reality.

   (John M. MacEachran memorial lecture series: 1976)
   Bibliography: p.
   Includes index.
   1. Cognition in children.   2. Children–Religious
life.   3. Perception in children.   I. Series.
BF723.C5E43   155.4'13   78-7351
ISBN 0-470-26376-8

Printed in the United States of America

Contents

Foreword   **vii**

Preface   **xi**

1. **Religious Development** **1**

   Introduction   1
   The Problem   3
   The Research   5
   Stage I (Usually Ages 5–7)   9
   Stage II (Usually Ages 7–9)   18
   Stage III (Usually Ages 10–12)   22
   The Child's Conception of Prayer   27

2. **Perceptual Development in Children** **47**

   Introduction   47
   Pictorial Measures of Perceptual Regulations   49
   Perceptual Development and Reading   75

3. Egocentrism **85**

   The Problem of Egocentrism   85
   Infancy   90
   Early Childhood   92
   The Concrete Operational Period   97
   The Formal Operational Period   117

Conclusion **129**

   References   **131**
   Author's Publications   **135**
   Subject Index   **153**

Foreword

It is a very great pleasure to introduce to you our Third MacEachran Memorial Lecturer, David Elkind. Dr. Elkind is a ULCA PhD, and he is currently Professor of Psychology and Education at the University of Rochester. He was formerly a member of the Psychology Department at the University of Denver.

As was the case for our first two MacEachran lecturers, Frank Geldard and Benton Underwood, Dr. Elkind is a man of vast accomplishments. Like most distinguished scientists, he has authored numerous technical articles in a wide variety of fields. A partial list of these fields would include cognitive development, educational psychology, social development, perception, personality development, adolescence, and moral development. Dr. Elkind is the author of advanced scholarly books, handbook chapters, and introductory textbooks in such areas as child development, education, Piaget's theory, and adolescence. Unlike most scientists, he has also found time to do an impressive amount of nontechnical writing, including a series of widely reputed biographical essays on famous psychologists that appeared originally in the *New York Times Magazine.*

Although it would be profitless to attempt to document all of Dr. Elkind's contributions to the many areas in which he has worked, there is one overriding contribution for which Dr. Elkind is perhaps best known among psychologists at large; specifically, this is his role as an exponent of Piaget's theory of cognitive development. Nowadays, Piaget's theory dominates research on cognitive development the way the white rat once dominated the study of learning. But it was not always so. Developmental psychologists are, as Sheldon White once observed, a pretty atheoretical lot, who basically want to know what the facts are. Consequently, we were, during the 1950s, somewhat less than enthusiastic about a theory as grandiose and difficult as Piaget's. In addition, the theory evolved from a research methodology that, in the spirit of Christian charity, may best be termed as *idiosyncratic.* The methodology spawns inevitable doubts about the replicability of the findings it generates.

For more than two decades, the result of much of Dr. Elkind's work has been to blunt the force of these two criticisms. With regard to replicability, Dr. Elkind, in a series of studies published in the early 1960s, was one of the first to demonstrate beyond reasonable doubt that key Piagetian findings on the development of concepts of quantity, number, kinship and so on were in fact replicable. Needless to say, this work helped to turn many Piaget doubters into Piaget researchers. Concerning the theory's intrinsic difficulty, Dr. Elkind has labored in papers, chapters, and books to spell out its basic meaning. Many of his expository writings not only amplify otherwise obscure ideas but they do so in a manner designed to fit the requirements of specialized audiences such as educators, child psychologists, and clinicians. Dr. Elkind's recent book, *Child development and education: A Piagetian perspective* (1976), is one of his latest efforts along these lines.

Thus, David Elkind is more than an interpreter of Jean Piaget; he is a student in the best sense of that term. He has attempted not only to grasp and communicate Piaget's difficult theory but also to build upon and extend it to different domains. It is that facet of his work that is represented in this book.

Focusing essentially on his own research and clinical observations, David Elkind — the clinician, researcher, and educator — has in these lectures both extended and further refined and defined the significance and utility of Piagetian concepts in understanding infant, child, and adolescent development.

In addition, these lectures represent the first comprehensive documentation and exposition of how classical Piagetian theory and methodology can be applied equally successfully in defining how children construct their reality across what would appear to be three phenotypically discrepant developmental "themes" — namely, religion, perception, and egocentrism. By eloquently elucidating the internal consistency of Piagetian principles across such seemingly diverse aspects of human development as well as by extending them to aspects of child and adolescent behavioral psychopathology, David Elkind has again led the way in sensitizing researchers, educators, and practitioners to "Piagetian perspectives."

These lectures will, most certainly, be a unique and very impressive contribution to the literature in child and developmental psychology.

For the MacEachran Memorial
Lecture Series Committee
Eugene C. Lechelt, Chairman
Charles J. Brainerd

Preface

It is a very great honor and privilege for me to give the Third Annual MacEachran Lectures. I am particularly pleased at being the first developmental psychologist to participate in this series and to be in the distinguished company of such psychologists as Frank A. Geldard, Benton J. Underwood, and John M. MacEachran. It has taken a long time, almost half a century, for developmental psychology to become a member in good standing of the scientific community. I therefore, take the invitation to deliver the MacEachran lectures not only as a recognition of personal achievement but much more as a recognition of the achievements of the discipline that I represent.

In preparing these lectures, I was placed in something of a dilemma. Our most recent work, on the construction of the self and self-differentiation in development, is very exciting but also still quite fragmentary. With so much yet to be done before an integrated presentation of the work is possible, I hesitated to inflict it upon you. Rather, what I have chosen to do is to present three lines of research that I have pursued over the years and for which there are established, as well as fresh, data.

One of these domains is religious development; another is perceptual development; and the third is the development of egocentrism. What the MacEachran lectures have permitted me to do, and what I have not done before, is to bring these three lines of research together and to show how they relate one to the other. So, though not all of the research I present is unfamiliar, the attempt at elaboration, integration, and systematization is new and, I hope, a step beyond where the material was before.

I have entitled these lectures *The child's reality: Three Developmental themes* for several different reasons. The first part of the title reflects the guiding aim of all my research — namely, to better understand how the child constructs reality out of his or her experiences with the environment. This aim clearly derives from the assumption that we can never know the environment in and of itself but only our reconstructions of it. My constructionist viewpoint as well as my research efforts derive of course from the work of Jean Piaget. It was Piaget who made the question of how the child constructs reality a stimulating one for North American psychologists. And Canadian psychologists — such as Adrien Pinard and Monique Laurendeau — were among the first on this side of the Atlantic to recognize the value of Piaget's research and theory.

The second part of the title, *Three developmental themes,* is a little more ambiguous. I seem to be captivated by the magic number three (perhaps because I have three sons), and it is used here in three different senses. First of all, it stands for the three different lines of research that I have pursued over the years. I have tried to study how children go about constructing the concepts of social institutions (namely their conceptions of their religious denominations and of prayer). Secondly, I have looked at how children go about constructing perceptual organizations (of parts and wholes, figure and ground, and so on). And finally, I have looked at the misunderstandings children construct about themselves and others (the egocentrism of different age levels). In short, the first meaning of "three developmental themes" is that of three different lines of research investigation.

But the "three themes" has a second significance as well. The three lines of research presented here also demonstrate three different research methods. In studying children's religious development, I employed Piaget's semiclinical method (a structured interview procedure), which is useful for exploring the changing contents of the child's thought. To study perceptual development, on the other hand, I sometimes made use of experimental procedures that are most appropriate for studying changes in mental processes and for isolating which processes are in play. Finally, the work on egocentrism represents the method of naturalistic observation, the delineation and labeling of the phenomena of everyday life.

To my mind, each of these methods is useful; and which one is used depends in part on the subject matter and in part on the state of development of the area to be studied. Perception, for example, is a well established field of inquiry; hence more advanced procedures such as experimentation are in order. Some work on religious development has been done but not a great deal; so more exploratory procedures, such as the semiclinical interview, seemed to be in order. And finally, because egocentrism (as I conceive it) has not yet been studied in a systematic way, a naturalistic approach appeared called for. But such an approach has eventually to be superseded by more systematic procedures. In this regard, I report a recent questionnaire study of egocentrism we have just completed that goes beyond the naturalistic observations.

Finally, there is a third meaning to the "three developmental themes" of this book's title. All of my research efforts have been aimed at demonstrating that the child's reality is different than that of adults, and in very special ways. First of all, the child's reality is neither preformed in the genes nor copied from the environment but is actively constructed by the child. Secondly, this constructive process is ongoing and continues throughout the human life cycle. Finally, the realities that are constructed at any point in the sequence of development are genuine constructions and cannot be reduced either to mental process or to empirical content; they always represent a creative union of the two. So, embedded in each of the three lines of research and the three methods of investigation that I describe are three more basic themes that are common to all developmental progressions. These more basic themes are that reality is a construction, that the process of constructing reality is continuous and that reality is always an irreducible amalgam of process and content of mind in confrontation with the environment.

THE CHILD'S REALITY:
Three Developmental Themes

Religious Development 1

INTRODUCTION

In contemporary psychology, religion is not a very popular topic, and it is rarely to be found in the index of any major textbook of introductory or developmental psychology. It was not always so, however; and around the turn of the century, religion was quite a respectable focus of psychological investigation. Indeed, such illustrious figures in the history of psychology as William James (1902) and G. Stanley Hall (1908) had much to say about religious experience and religious development. And a student shared by both of these men, William Starbuck, carried out the classic studies of religious conversion in adolescents (1900).

What happened, then, to cause this about-face with respect to American psychology's interest in religion? Well, many different circumstances were probably working in combination. For one thing, World War I happened. American psychology had until that time taken its lead from German psychology. And German psychology, at least some parts of it, was heavily mentalistic and hence accepting of studies of religious thought and behavior. But World War I made Americans hostile to Germany, and it made American psychologists hostile to German psychology. American psychology turned away from mentalism, and hence from religious phenomena, in part as a negative reaction to German psychology.

The German influence was replaced by English associationism and Russian reflexology. Both systems were no-nonsense, empiricist approaches to human behavior that eschewed anything mystical – including religion. After the war, American psychology wanted to be scientific in the sense of physics and not in the sense of German mentalism. Science, at this point, meant experimentation and quantification. Because it is hard to control and manipulate human behavior, many American psychologists turned to the study of animals.

As behaviorism took over American psychology, it aligned itself with science and put itself in opposition to religion. Religion was regarded as a false path to knowledge, whereas science was regarded as the true path. Psychoanalysis, then becoming popular in America, also contributed to this denigration of religion by labeling it as a kind of neurosis. And, although never a major factor in American life, communism did have a big appeal to intellectuals in the Depression days. And the communist credo that "religion is the opiate of the people" contributed to the scientific, if not the popular, derogation of religion.

There are some evidences of a change in contemporary psychology and social science generally.

Religion as a topic of study is becoming popular on campuses; and among scientists, the negative attitudes toward religion — though still present — seem diminished. Perhaps this new attitude is attributable in part to the fact that science and technology have created many human problems for which there are no simple scientific answers. The scientist, faced with moral dilemmas about biological or nuclear research, must look beyond science for guidance. The scientist's dilemma may make him or her more sympathetic to the provision of moral guidance that religions have always offered.

Quite apart from changing attitudes, however, religion regarded as a social institution, rather than as an opponent of science, has always been a legitimate subject for psychological investigation. As a social institution, religion poses the problem — to the developmentalist at any rate — as to how children assimilate and become part of that institution. It is from that standpoint, the standpoint of children's progressive assimilation of institutional religion, that my coworkers and I undertook the study of children's conceptions of their religious denominations and of prayer.

THE PROBLEM

One way to pose the problem of children and religion is to ask how children go about acquiring the concepts of institutional religion. By engaging children in conversation about the concepts of institutional religion, one can trace how these ideas are progressively understood. In this regard the concepts of institutional religion are no different from the concepts of mathematics or science that Piaget (1950) studied from the standpoint of their progressive assimilation by children. This approach reflects John Dewey's (1902) conception of the function of collective knowledge in education — that it be used not as a curriculum to be taught but rather as a guide to observing and directing the child's intellectual explorations.

Before proceeding, it should be said that this way of attacking the question of the child and religion begs the question of the child's spontaneous religiosity. Are there, for example, behaviors, attitudes, or feelings that are religious from the outset and quite independent of experience and training? Unfortunately, the problem is as much definitional as it is factual. It depends on what one regards as essential to religion: love, belief in a particular dogma, a sense of awe and reverence, and so on. As far as I have been able to determine, there is no generally accepted definition of the psychological components of religion (Elkind, 1971).

To be sure, children have propensities that resemble religious concepts. Young children, for example, regard their parents as all powerful and as all knowing, and they regard all important figures as godlike (Bovet, 1928). One young man, on hearing of the brutal killing of John F. Kennedy, asked in bewilderment, "Are they going to shoot God next?" But is the belief in someone who is all powerful and all knowing a religious belief? Does there not have to be dogma for true religious conviction?

Accordingly, it may be useful to distinguish between *personal* religion on the one hand and *institutional* religion on the other. Personal religion would be the feelings, concepts, and attitudes that children manifest and that resemble those found in persons displaying institutional religion — belief in a deity. But in the case of the children, the feelings, attitudes, and concepts may be experienced in relation to living persons, to nature, or even toward animals. Personal religion is of great interest but is difficult to study. In my work I have concentrated on how children progressively reconstruct institutional religion — the beliefs, practices, and dogmas of established religions.

THE RESEARCH

Every child who is exposed to religious teaching eventually arrives at an understanding of what it means to belong to a particular religious group, i.e., a conception of his or her religious denomination or identity. The question arises, however, as to whether this conception of religious identity is entirely due to the effects of religious instruction or whether its formation is determined, at least in part, by developmental factors. According to Jean Piaget, for example, conceptions develop in a necessary sequence of stages that are related to age. At each developmental level, in Piaget's view, the products of thought are determined by the interaction of developmental and experiential factors. Piaget, however, has not explored the growth of religious conceptions, and the course of their development remains to be demonstrated.

It was the need for such a demonstration that led the present writer to study the growth of religious identity conceptions among children of different faiths. Three investigations were carried out — one with Jewish (Elkind, 1961), one with Catholic (Elkind, 1962), and one with Congregational Protestant (Elkind, 1963) youngsters. If Piaget's view of conceptual development holds for religious conceptions, then one might expect the conceptions for each group to reflect both the operations that they share in common and the experiences wherein they differ. In general the results of the studies were in agreement with the Piagetian position, and the development of religious identity conceptions seemed to mirror the interaction of developmental and environmental factors. These studies were published separately and now, for the first time, I summarize the results of the three investigations and elaborate on some of the similarities and differences among the three religious groups.

Before summarizing the results of the studies, however, a brief description of the method by which they were obtained may help orient the reader for what is to come. The method employed was the semiclinical interview devised by Piaget (1929). It will be recalled that this method requires a set of novel questions — designed to elicit spontaneous thought — that serve as the starting point for an interview-type discussion aimed at clarifying the child's initial responses. The questions used in the denominational conception studies were formulated on the assumption that such a conception consists of at least four components: (a) ideas regarding the extent of membership in the child's religious group; (b) ideas regarding the external or internal evidences of religious group differences; (c) ideas regarding the common property or properties shared by all religious group members; and finally, (d) some ideas about the possibility of multiple (nonreligious) group membership.

In order to explore the child's thought in each of these four areas of conceptualization, the following six questions were devised. Of these questions, two dealt with the extent of religious group membership: (a) Are you a _____? Is your family _____? Are all boys and girls in the world _____? and (b) can a cat or a dog be a _____? To disclose the child's awareness of external signs of religiosity, the following question was asked: (c) How can you tell a person is a _____? Of the remaining three questions, two dealt with the properties common to all members of a particular religious group: (d) What is a _____? and (e) How do you become a _____? The final question dealt with the problem of multiple group membership: (f) Can you be an American and a _____ at the same time? These questions were the starting point for a discussion in which the examiner encouraged the children to amplify and clarify their answers.

Close to 800 children participated in the investigations, and with the exception of some of the Protestant children, all the subjects were individually interviewed by the writer. Of the 790 children seen, 210 were Jewish, 280 were Catholic, and 300 were Congregational Protestant. The Jewish children ranged in age from 5 to 11; the Catholic children from 6 to 12; and the Protestant children from 6 to 14. With the exception of the Protestant children, there were at least 30 at each age level within the age ranges indicated.

The results of the interviews were evaluated by means of Piaget's (1929) criteria for determining a true developmental sequence. These criteria were: (a) uniformity of responses among children at one or more adjacent age levels; (b) the presence of adherences (remnants of ideas appropriate to young children among the older children) and anticipations (suggestions of ideas appropriate to older children among the younger subjects); and (c) movement with age in the direction of more abstract and adultlike conceptualization. All of these criteria were met by the replies given by each denominational group, and the replies were therefore classed according to developmental stages. In what follows, each stage is taken up first from the point of view of the four components of religious identity conceptualization and then from the point of view of denominational group differences. For those concerned with the statistical comparison of the groups, Tables 1.1 through 1.4 give the percent of children from each group who answered a particular question at a particular level. Only four of the six questions are represented in these tables, because the responses to the other two were too varied to be easily grouped into stages.

STAGE I (USUALLY AGES 5–7)

At the first stage, children had a global, undifferentiated conception of their religious identity. These youngsters knew that denominational terms referred to persons and that such terms related to the God concept. But when they were forced by the examiner's questions to break down this global conception and to state its particular referents, they chose at random among national, racial, and ethnic qualities. This global, undifferentiated quality of thinking permeated all four components of religious identity conceptualization.

Extent of Denominational Group Membership

Children at the first stage already had an idea that denominational terms were not all-inclusive categories; but when they were forced to rationalize these ideas by the examiner's questions, they erected racial, national, and geographic boundaries.

Bob (6–5) (ages in years and months): Are all boys and girls in the world Protestant? "No." Why not? "Some are Irish, and some are Russian."

Lin (5–10): Are you Jewish? "Yes." Is your family Jewish? "Yes, well all except my dog, he's a *French* poodle."

TABLE 1.1

Percentage[a] of Replies to the Question, "Are all boys and girls in the world, _____?" Given by Jewish (J), Catholic (C) and Protestant (P) Children for Three Developmental Stages and For 8 Age Levels

N			Age level	Stage								
				I			II			III		
J	C	P		J	C	P	J	C	P	J	C	P
30	0	0	5	60	0	0	13	0	0	–	0	0
30	37	18	6	60	65	75	40	35	–	–	–	–
30	41	0	7	23	38	0	67	72	0	10	–	0
30	38	42	8	17	15	3	63	80	86	20	5	11
30	44	32	9	3	6	–	74	71	81	23	23	19
30	44	44	10	7	2	–	17	66	50	76	32	50
30	40	29	11	–	–	–	33	53	42	67	47	58
0	37	60	12	0	3	–	0	32	25	0	68	75

[a]Percentages may not total 100 because not every child questioned gave a scorable reply.

TABLE 1.2

Percentage[a] of Replies to the Question, "Can a dog or a cat be a _____?"
Given by Jewish (J), Catholic (C) and Protestant (P) Children for
Three Developmental Stages and For 8 Age Levels

N			Age level	Stage								
				I			II			III		
J	C	P		J	C	P	J	C	P	J	C	P
30	0	0	5	60	0	0	13	0	0	—	0	0
30	37	18	6	60	65	55	40	35	20	—	—	—
30	41	0	7	16	38	0	77	69	0	7	3	0
30	38	42	8	10	5	6	77	85	91	13	10	3
30	44	32	9	—	2	3	93	59	84	7	39	13
30	44	44	10	3	—	—	77	66	83	20	34	17
30	40	29	11	—	—	—	57	58	71	43	42	29
0	37	60	12	0	—	—	0	32	25	0	68	75

[a]Percentages may not total 100 because not every child questioned gave a scorable reply.

TABLE 1.3

Percentage[a] of Replies to the Question, "What is a _____?" Given by Jewish (J), Catholic (C) and Protestant (P) Children for Three Developmental Stages and For 8 Age Levels

Age level	N			Stage I			Stage II			Stage III		
	J	C	P	J	C	P	J	C	P	J	C	P
5	30	0	0	50	0	0	7	0	0	–	0	0
6	30	37	18	70	62	20	30	38	5	–	–	–
7	30	41	0	23	28	0	67	69	0	10	3	0
8	30	38	42	27	13	11	60	63	39	13	24	33
9	30	44	32	3	2	9	54	64	41	43	34	34
10	30	44	44	–	–	3	23	52	33	77	48	58
11	30	40	29	–	–	–	27	23	25	73	77	75
12	0	37	60	0	–	2	0	16	32	0	84	66

[a]Percentages may not total 100 because not every child questioned gave a scorable reply.

TABLE 1.4

Percentage[a] of Replies to the Question, "Can you be an American and a _____ at the same time?"

Given by Jewish (J), Catholic (C) and Protestant (P) Children for Three Developmental Stages and For 8 Age Levels

N			Age level	Stage								
				I			II			III		
J	C	P		J	C	P	J	C	P	J	C	P
30	0	0	5	63	0	0	17	0	0	—	0	0
30	37	18	6	74	62	20	26	38	5	—	—	—
30	41	0	7	23	28	0	77	72	0	—	—	—
30	38	42	8	10	11	11	87	89	39	3	—	33
30	44	32	9	—	2	9	90	82	41	10	9	34
30	44	44	10	—	2	3	67	84	33	33	14	58
30	40	29	11	—	—	—	60	64	25	40	36	75
0	37	60	12	0	—	2	0	62	32	0	38	66

[a]Percentages may not total 100 because not every child questioned gave a scorable reply.

13

First-stage children's awareness of the limited inclusiveness of denominational terms was also shown by their response to the "dog and cat" question. As with the first question, however, their explanations of this limited inclusiveness revealed their confusion as to the specific referents of denominational terms.

Lee (6–2): Can a dog or cat be a Catholic? "No." Why not? "They are not a person, they are animals." How are animals different from people? "They walk on four legs."

Mar (5–1): Can a dog or a cat be a Protestant? "No." Why not? "Because it's a dog." But why can't it be a Protestant? "It goes bowwow."

It is clear from these replies that first-stage children judged that a particular denominational term did not refer to all persons nor to any animals. First-stage children were, however, unable to correctly explain their judgments.

External Signs of Religious Group Membership

In general, first-stage children had little or no idea as to how a Protestant, Catholic, or Jew might be recognized. They either said that they did not know or gave fanciful answers:

Bob (6–3): How can you tell a person is Jewish? "I don't know."

Hal (5–10): How can you tell a person is Protestant? "The way they talk." How do you mean? "They have a little black cap sorta."

These replies gave further evidence of first-stage children's confusion regarding even the most concrete referents of a denominational term. This confusion was present despite the fact that these children knew the term applied to a limited number of persons and not to animals.

The Common Property Connoted by Denominational Terms

The replies to questions dealing with the property common to denominational group members complemented those already obtained. Once more the young children demonstrated their awareness that denominational terms referred to people but also their confusion about specific referents of the terms.

Jay (6–1): What is a Catholic? "A person." How is he different from a Protestant? "I don't know."

Sid (6–3): What is a Jew? "A person." How is a Jewish person different from a Catholic person? "Cause some people have black hair and some people have blonde."

A new facet of denominational conceptions was revealed by children's answers to the question about becoming a member of the group. Replies to this question indicated that even at the first stage, children already associated denominational terms with the God concept.

Lon (6–1): How do you become Protestant? "God makes you it."

Tom (6—1): How do you become Jewish? "God makes you Jewish."

First-stage children knew that a denominational term pertained to God, but they regarded God as the "Maker" of their denomination as if it were some real object or quality.

Awareness of Multiple Group Membership

Replies to the question regarding multiple group membership made it at once clear that the first-stage children did not distinguish between religious and nonreligious class designations. And, as in the answers to the previous question, they displayed a kind of nominal realism and seemed to believe that denominational terms had physical existence. Consequently, these children argued that multiple group membership was impossible for physical reasons — namely, that one thing couldn't be two things at the same time.

Lea (6—2): Can you be a Catholic and an American at the same time? "No." Why not? "I don't know." Are you a Catholic? "Yes." Are you an American? "No."

Ed (6—2): Can you be a Jew and an American at the same time? "No." Why not? "You can't have two (names)."

For these children there was a lack of differentiation between national and religious designations but also a reification of the terms. As one child expressed it, he could be both at the same time "only if we move." At the first stage, then, the conception of religious identity was global and undifferentiated without clear awareness of the specific referents of denominational terms.

Denominational Group Similarities and Differences

Despite the quite different backgrounds and experiences of the children, the uniformity of responses at this age level was striking. There were, nevertheless, group differences even at this early stage. For one thing, the Protestant children were far behind both the Catholic and the Jewish children in awareness of denominational group membership. This may be due in part to the fact that the term *Protestant* is a second-order (including many subclasses) concept, whereas the terms *Catholic* and *Jewish* are both first-order concepts. Inasmuch as second-order concepts are more difficult to learn than those of the first order, this conceptual difficulty might account for the conceptual lag among Protestant children. It should be said, however, that when Protestant youngsters were asked whether they were "Congregational" (a first-order concept), they were equally at sea. The delay in the Protestant child's awareness of his or her denomination is thus probably not entirely due to difficulty in conceptualizing it. In addition, this delay may reflect a fundamental difference in the age of onset and intensity of religious education between the denominational groups. In this regard, it needs also to be commented that at this age level it was the Catholic and Jewish children who displayed the largest reservoir of religious knowledge.

STAGE II (USUALLY AGES 7–9)

By the age of 7 to 9, some rather remarkable progress was made in the conceptualization of religious identity. This progress can best be measured in comparison with what was known at the first stage. In contrast to the first-stage child who knew only that the denominational terms referred to persons, the second-stage child knew *what* persons were designated. The second-stage child accomplished this differentiation because he or she had abstracted certain concrete referents, primarily actions, characteristic of different denominational groups. It was the abstraction of concrete referent properties of denominational terms that was the outstanding characteristic of the second stage.

Extent of Denominational Group Membership

The awareness of the limits of denominational group membership among second-stage children was reflected in their spontaneous use of other denominational terms in response to the first question.

Hal (8–7): Are all boys and girls in the world Catholic? "No." Why? "Some are Jews, and some are Protestant." Anything else? "No."

Paul (7–3): Are all boys and girls in the world Protestant? "No." Why not? "Because some are Catholic, and some are Jewish." How do you know? "They live in my block."

Answers to the dog–cat question revealed a similar differentiation, only now with respect to concrete behaviors in addition to the differentiation between denominational terms revealed by the answers to the first question.

Herb (9–2): Can a dog or a cat be a Catholic? "No." Why not? "Because he can't go to church or receive the sacraments, stuff like that."

Stu (8–3): Can a dog or a cat be a Jew? "No." Why not? "They are not human." What difference does that make? "They can't go to the synagogue or say the prayers."

It is interesting to note that the spontaneous use of different denominational terms appears at the same time as evidence for the abstraction of criteria for discriminating between their referents. This correlation would seem to reflect the close connection between thought and language; i.e., a child will spontaneously use a term when it has meaning (a reference base) for him or her.

External Signs of Religious Group Membership

Second-stage children used religious actions not only for excluding animals from religious group membership, but also as distinguishing signs of particular religious group membership.

Nor (9–4): How can you tell a person is a Protestant? "The way they act." How do you mean? "You can tell by the church they go to."

Will (8–2): How can you tell a person is Catholic? "If you see them go into a Catholic church."

These children had, it was clear, arrived at a concrete means of recognizing membership in a particular denomination.

The Common Property Connoted by Denominational Terms

As might be expected from the foregoing discussion, second-stage children regarded particular actions as the property shared by all members of a particular denomination.

Al (7–9): What is a Jew? "A person who goes to Temple and to Hebrew School."

Herb (9–12): What is a Catholic? "He goes to mass every Sunday and goes to Catholic School."

The same action emphasis appeared in response to the other common property question.

Will (8–2): How do you become a Catholic? "You get baptized, the priest throws water over you [*sic!*]."

Beth (7–1): How do you become a Protestant? "By going to a Protestant church."

Concrete action thus permeated the religious thinking of these children and served as a source of answers to all religious questions.

Awareness of Multiple
Group Membership

Second-stage children, in contrast to youngsters at
the first stage, were able to grasp the notion of
multiple group membership. But the understanding
of this notion was built upon the awareness of actions as the distinguishing feature of categorical
terms.

El (9–7): Can you be a Protestant and an American at the same time? "Yes." How is that possible?
"Because I live in America and was baptized."

Pr (7–8): Can you be a Jew and an American at
the same time? "Yes." How is that possible? "Because you live in America and are an American Jew."

For second-stage children, the discovery and abstraction of religious actions was the magic key to
the understanding of religious terms; and it was sufficient for recognizing the extent of denominational
membership, for recognizing individual members of
a denomination, for giving meaning to the denominational term itself, and for recognizing the com-
patibility of multiple group membership. The
limitation of the action criterion, however, appears
when the responses of the third-stage children are
considered.

Denominational Group Similarities
and Differences

Once again the similarities between the groups
were more striking than the differences. There was

one difference, however, that deserves to be noted. It appeared in responses to the question, "How do you become a _____?" Far more Jewish than either Catholic or Protestant children said that they were Jewish because their families were. Christian children, on the other hand, attributed their religious identity to some form of church activity. This difference may reflect the emphasis in the Jewish religion on the importance of ritual observances carried out in the home and the fact that Jewish religion and Jewish culture are not really separable.

STAGE III (USUALLY AGES 10–12)

Children at the third stage displayed a new level of thinking about their religious denominations. If the second stage could be characterized as one in which action held sway, then the third stage would have to be designated as one of *reflection*. At the third stage, children no longer looked for manifestations of religious identity in the person's outward behavior, but rather they sought it in the evidence of his or her innermost beliefs and convictions.

Extent of Denominational Group Membership

It was noted earlier that the spontaneous use of certain terms coincided with the awareness of the meaning of those terms. This was true in relation to the child's use of the term *religion*, which did not appear spontaneously until the third stage — coincident with the discovery of belief as the core of religious identity.

Bob (11–12): Are all boys and girls in the world Catholic? "No, some belong to other religions."

Jeb (10–6): Are all boys and girls in the world Protestant? "No." Why is that? "God made all different religions."

The other side of the reflective coin is revealed in the responses to the dog–cat question.

Bill (12–0): Can a dog or a cat be Protestant? "No, because they don't have a brain or an intellect."

Sid (11–4): Can a dog or a cat be Jewish? "No." Why not? "Because they are not human and would not understand a religion."

The use by third-stage children of the terms *intellect* and *understanding* indicated that they had abstracted their own mental processes and used such processes as the criteria of religious identity. At the same time, this higher level of abstraction also permitted the formation of the third-level class conception of *religion*. Again, the spontaneous use of new terms such as *intelligence* and *think* reflects the connection between conceptual development and language usage.

External Signs of Religious
Group Membership

In contrast to second-stage children, many third-stage youngsters said there was no (external) way you could tell that a person was a Catholic, a

Protestant, or a Jew. This reflected their awareness that religious identity was an inner and not an outer manifestation. The answers of those children who did reply to the question pointed in the same direction as the negative answers.

Claire (11–7): How can you tell a person is a Protestant? "Because they are free to repent and to pray to God in their own way."

The Common Property Connoted by Denominational Terms

After the foregoing discussion of the third stage, it might be expected that children at this stage would find the property shared by all denominational group members to be such things as beliefs and convictions. This was, in fact, what was observed.

Bill (12–0): What is a Catholic? "A person who believes in the truth of the Roman Catholic Church."

Sid (10–4): What is a Jew? "A person who believes in one God and does not believe in the New Testament."

A similar theme ran through the replies of third-stage youngsters to the other question under this category.

Tom (11–7): How do you become a Catholic? "You gotta study your religion, study the catechism, receive communion and first confession."

Beth (12–5): How do you become a Protestant? "Well, you are baptized first and worship in the Protestant way and follow Protestant rules."

At this stage, religious membership meant more than attending church; it signified thought, study, and the observance of a moral and an ethical code.

Awareness of Multiple Group Membership

As one might anticipate, third-stage children were often amused by the question regarding multiple group membership. The level of their explanations was in keeping with the high level of abstraction that has already been demonstrated as characteristic of this stage.

Bob (11–12): Can you be a Catholic and an American at the same time? "Yes." How is that possible? "They are two different things — American is a nationality; Catholic is a religion."

Bert (12–5): Can you be a Jew and an American at the same time? "Yes, because in America you have the right to be any religion you want."

At the third stage, the lines between religion and nationality are clearly drawn — not on the basis of behavior — as at the second stage — but rather on abstract categorical grounds.

Denominational Group Similarities and Differences

Once more the similarity in level of conceptualization among the three groups has to be remarked on as evidence of a developmental stage in religious growth. On the other hand, there were group differences. One of the most interesting of these was the way in which children answered the question, "What is a _____?" To this question, the Catholic children often replied by stressing the practices and creeds of their church. Protestant children, on the other hand, often defined their identity negatively by placing themselves in opposition to Catholic doctrine. The same was frequently true for Jewish children, who often defined themselves in contradistinction to Christian dogma (i.e., the New Testament). Put differently, this suggests that Protestant and Jewish children conceive their religious identity relatively, in contrast to other religions; whereas the Catholic children conceive their identity absolutely and within the confines of their own church.

The results of the present study have shown that before the age of 11–12, most children are unable to understand religious concepts as they are understood by adults. In addition, the results have shown that children spontaneously give meanings to religious terms that reflect their unique world view. This result is not surprising, and stories about such spontaneous meanings given to religious terms by children are legion. One little girl from Connecticut, for example, was overheard reciting the Lord's Prayer in the following manner: "Our Father who art in New Haven, Harold be thy name"; and many children go to the zoo expecting to see "the cross-eyed bear" (the cross I bear) they heard about in church. Such examples could be multiplied; but together with the evidence presented in the preceding pages, it should suffice to show that most children fail to understand abstract religious expressions prior to adolescence and that they interpret such expressions within the limits of their own levels of comprehension.

These results, then, give evidence in support of the three underlying themes of these lectures. They show that the child's conceptions are constructed (neither innate nor simply learned). This is true because if they were innate, they would not change; and if they were simply learned, they would not differ so radically from adult conceptions. The data also show that the process of construction is continuous from early childhood through adolescence. And finally, the data show that at each level, mental constructions reflect the interaction of development and experience. We can demonstrate these same three themes with data from the child's conception of prayer.

THE CHILD'S CONCEPTION OF PRAYER[1]

The general aim of the present study was to trace empirically the development of the prayer concept as it evolves in the elementary school child. More particularly, our concern was with the developmental changes that occur in the form and content of the prayer concept and in the fantasies and feelings associated with it.

[1]This study was done in collaboration with Diane Long and Bernard Spilka.

Method

Subjects

The subjects for the study were 160 boys and girls between the ages of 5 and 12. Of these, 132 attended one of two private schools in suburban Denver. The remaining 28 were obtained directly from homes in the middle-class suburban neighborhood. The children were selected so that there were 20 at each year of age. They were divided approximately equally between boys and girls.

As a group, the children came from an above-average socioeconomic level. Much variation in amount and kind of religious training was represented. Subjects were distributed among religious groups as follows: 51 Episcopalian, 23 Jewish, 21 Presbyterian, 13 Roman Catholic, 7 Methodist, 6 Congregational, 6 Lutheran, 1 Unitarian, and 32 unknown.

Interview Materials

In order to explore developmental changes in the *form* of the prayer concept, semistructured questions were employed:

1. "Do you pray?", "Does your family pray?", "Do all boys and girls in the world pray?"
2. "Do dogs and cats pray?"
3. "What is a prayer?"
4. "Can you pray for more than one thing?"

5. "What must you do if your prayer is answered?"

6. "If it is not?"

To explore developmental changes in the *content* of children's prayer activity and the fantasies and affects associated with such activities, four incomplete sentences and two open-ended questions were employed. The incomplete sentences were:

1. "I usually pray when . . ."
2. "Sometimes I pray for . . ."
3. "When I pray, I feel . . ."
4. "When I see someone praying, I . . ."

The direct questions aimed at eliciting some fantasy material associated with prayer were:

5. "Where do prayers come from?"
6. "Where do prayers go?"

Procedure

Each child was individually interviewed. To orient the child and to build rapport, he or she was first shown two pictures in which families were engaged in prayer, then asked to describe what was going on in the scenes. The semistructured questions were then introduced, and these were followed by the incomplete sentences and the direct questions. Every effort was made to encourage the child to respond freely and spontaneously during the course of the interview.

Analyses of the Data

The children's responses to the interview materials were first analyzed qualitatively and then quantitatively so as to test statistically impressions gained from a subjective reading of the protocols.

Differentiation and Abstraction: Prayer Conception Scores. Replies to the six semistructured questions were examined for uniformities among age groups and for age trends. For the most part, the responses seemed to fall into the three stages found in the previous study: (a) a global undifferentiated stage; (b) a concrete differentiated stage; and (c) a differentiated abstract stage. These were scored as though along a single dimension, with scores, respectively, of 0, 1, and 2. A verbal formulation of the criteria for each category was then made, and these criteria were submitted to two judges (school psychologists) not involved with the study. Each of the judges and one of us (DL) then independently scored 25 protocols chosen at random from all age levels. The interjudge reliabilities, obtained by means of a randomized blocks analysis of variance described by Winer (1962, p. 130), varied from .92 to 1.00 for all questions. The internal consistency reliability of the coded responses for individual children and across age levels was .90.

Content of Prayer. Children's replies to the incomplete sentences and direct questions were grouped according to content categories, and the percentage of responses in each category for each age level was then tabulated. Each child was scored according to whether or not he or she mentioned each category. Thus, if a child responded that he prayed for his mother, his father, his sister, and his brother, he was given only a single point for a response in the "family" category. If, on the other hand, she replied that she prayed for her grandmother and her dog, she was given two scores — one point for the "family" category and the other for the "pets" category. In short, it was the number of different categories mentioned rather than the number of elements within a particular category that determined the child's score. Since the number of responses given by children at the different age levels varied widely, it seemed most reasonable to consider these responses in relation to the total given at each age level, that is, in terms of percentages rather than in terms of absolute numbers. Because placing these responses in categories was a routine procedure, no assessment of the reliability of the classification was attempted.

Results

Differentiation and Abstraction:
Prayer Conception Scores

The mean scores for the six interview questions and for all age levels are given in Table 1.5. A multifactor analysis of variance for repeated measures (Table 1.6) revealed that differences between prayer

TABLE 1.5
Means and Standard Deviations for Prayer Conception Scores
for 8 Age Levels and 6 Prayer Questions

Age Levels		Questions						Across Questions
		1	2	3	4	5	6	
5	Mn	.25	.45	0	.25	.10	.15	.20
	SD	.54	.50	0	.43	.30	.35	.42
6	Mn	.55	.80	.30	.80	.30	.75	.58
	SD	.59	.40	.46	.60	.56	.70	.60
7	Mn	.95	1.15	.80	.90	.45	1.00	.87
	SD	.38	.57	.51	.43	.67	.71	.60
8	Mn	1.25	1.20	1.05	1.00	1.00	1.10	1.09
	SD	.43	.60	.38	.45	.77	.77	.54
9	Mn	1.45	1.50	1.60	1.35	1.20	1.65	1.45
	SD	.50	.50	.49	.48	.51	.65	.54
10	Mn	1.50	1.55	1.60	1.60	1.30	1.80	1.52
	SD	.50	.50	.49	.49	.46	.40	.50
11	Mn	1.60	1.55	1.65	1.90	1.65	1.65	1.66
	SD	.49	.74	.50	.30	.50	.50	.47
11–12	Mn	1.90	1.65	1.85	1.85	1.90	1.95	1.84
	SD	.30	.50	.35	.35	.30	.22	.36
Across	Mn	1.18	1.23	1.11	1.21	.99	1.26	
Age	SD	.71	.64	.77	.70	.81	.77	

conception scores at the successive age levels were significant beyond the .01 level ($F = 92.47$).

Application of the Scheffé (Table 1.7) test for comparison of any two age levels (Winer, 1962) suggested five more or less distinct age level clusterings. Age 5 was clearly separate from the other groupings and seemed to represent the clearest example of the global undifferentiated stage. Age levels 6 and 7 years also seemed to stand apart and to represent a transitional stage between the global and concrete differentiated levels of conceptualization. The 8-year-old group stood alone and might be regarded as representative of an unmixed concrete differentiated stage. Children aged 9 to 11 again seemed to form a transitional stage, this time between the concrete and abstract differentiated periods. The 12-year-old group stood relatively alone and appeared to be a more or less "pure" representation of the abstract differentiated stage.

The statistical analysis also revealed that some of the questions were "easier" than the others in the sense that more advanced replies were given to some questions than to others. (In Table 1.6, $F = 7.23$, $p < .01$.) For children at the transitional stages, the difficulty of the questions probably helped to determine the level of the response. Sex differences were also present but followed no consistent pattern and therefore were not interpreted.

In order to make the foregoing statistical summary concrete and to reveal some of the richness of the children's replies, illustrative examples of replies given at the various stages of conceptualization are presented below.

TABLE 1.6
Analysis of Variance of Prayer Conception Scores for 6 Prayer Questions and 8 Age Levels (*N* = 160)

Source	df	Sum of Squares	Mean Sq.	F	P
Between S	(159)	(343.47)	(2.16)		
Age	7	278.32	39.76	92.47	.01
Error	152	65.16	.43		
Within S	(800)	(192.50)	(.24)		
Questions	5	7.93	1.59	7.23	.01
A x Q	35	14.87	.42	1.91	.01
Error	760	169.70	.22		
Total	959	535.97			

TABLE 1.7
Scheffé Test[1] on Mean Abstraction Scores for Comparing Any Two Age Levels (Difference Scores in Body of Table)

Age Levels	Means	6	7	8	9	10	11	11–12
		(.58)	(.87)	(1.09)	(1.45)	(1.52)	(1.66)	(1.84)
5	(.20)	.38*	.67**	.89**	1.25**	1.32**	1.46**	1.64**
6	(.58)		.29	.51**	.87**	.94**	1.08**	1.26**
7	(.87)			.22	.56**	.65**	.79**	.97**
8	(1.09)				.36**	.43**	.57**	.75**
9	(1.45)					.07	.21	.39**
10	(1.52)						.14	.32*
11	(1.66)							.18

[1]Critical differences (p .05) = .324; (p .01) = .363.

Let * indicate difference is significant at .05; ** indicate difference significant at the .01 level.

Stage 1 (ages 5—7). At this stage, the children had only a vague and indistinct notion of prayer. Although they had a dim awareness that prayers were somehow linked with the term *God* and with certain learned formulae such as, "Now I lay me down to sleep," there was little real comprehension of the meaning of prayer. Some examples of this level of response are given below:

Nancy (5—11): What is a prayer? "A prayer is about God, rabbits, dogs, and fairies and deer, and Santa Claus and turkeys and pheasants, and Jesus and Mary and Mary's little baby."

Carol (5—8): What is a prayer? "A prayer is God bless people who want to say God bless. Now I lay me down to sleep . . ."

Children at the first stage, who were unclear as to the nature of prayer, tended to be equally unclear (individual consistency of level of response = .90) about whether dogs or cats could pray. If they thought of prayer as something associated with people, they said dogs and cats did not pray; whereas if they thought of it as something to do with speech, they argued that dogs and cats could pray, out of the childish belief that animals could talk. The choices were arbitrary, and the same child sometimes gave both a "no" and a "yes" answer without sensing any contradictions in his or her reply.

Since at the first stage, the concept of prayer was not yet differentiated by the child, he or she tended to feel that all boys and girls in the world really did pray and that they did so for a variety of amorphous and diffuse reasons.

Carol (5–3): Do all boys and girls in the world pray? "Yes, because they want to pray, and they want to pray to God." In response to the question, "Can you pray for more than one thing?", first-stage children seemed to guess at random and could give no rational explanation for their judgments.

Stage 2 (ages 7–9).   At the second stage, the prayer concept had clearly emerged from its previous undifferentiated state. Prayer was now conceived in terms of particular and appropriate activities, they were also concrete. At this stage, children never rose above the actual behaviors associated with prayer to its mental and affective aspects, which – to older child and adult – are its essence.

Jimmy (7–5): What is a prayer? "That we should have water, food, rain, and snow. It's something you ask God for – water, food, rain, and snow."

The identification of prayer with a particular form of activity, verbal requests, helped the child to recognize that pets could not pray. Dogs and cats were excluded from being able to pray, because they could not talk. One might say that at this stage the child mistook the form of prayer (its verbal component) for its substance (the thoughts and feelings associated with it).

The association of prayer with a particular activity also helped children to recognize that not all children in the world prayed. This recognition, however, was based on very concrete, personalized grounds. If not all children pray, this was explained by such things as "they forget" or "they are too sleepy" or because "they don't want anything" or simply because "they don't like to pray." With the notion that prayer involved activity, there was also the apparent corollary notion that this was a volitional activity about which one had a choice. Also coupled with this concrete notion of prayer was a modified view of God's omnipotence. When asked whether they could pray for more than one thing, children at the second stage indicated that God had a limited capacity to do things and that not everyone could be served completely and at once.

Stage 3 (ages 9–12).   At about the age of 9 or 10, and increasingly thereafter, prayer emerged as a type of private conversation with God, involving things not talked about with other people. Implicit in the replies at this stage was a distinction, which seldom if ever occurred in younger children, between what one *thinks* and what one *says*.

Dell (10–6): What is a prayer? "Prayer is a way to communicate with God." Communicate with God? "To ask him forgiveness, to ask him if something would go right when it's going wrong." Can you tell me more about that . . . ? "Well, sometimes you just want to talk to somebody, you just can always go to God and talk to Him."

Third-stage children also recognized that prayer involved the nonmaterial mental activities such as thought and belief. Dogs and cats were said not to be able to pray, because "they're not that smart" or because "they don't know that much." At the third stage, then, the essential aspect of prayer was a covert mental, rather than an overt motor, activity.

This new level of conceptualization was also revealed in the reasons the third-stage children gave for why all children in the world did not pray. In contrast to younger children, who simply generalized from their own personal experience ("they are too lazy," "forget," etc.), third-stage children looked upon prayer as but one aspect of a system of beliefs that was not shared by people all over the world. They thus explained that not all children pray, because some "do not believe in God" or because "they don't know about the Christian religion." The notion of prayer thus became not only more abstract but also more circumscribed, in the sense that it was now seen not as a universal human activity but rather as an activity associated with and derived from a particular belief system.

Summary. This in brief, then, is the evolution that the form of the prayer concept takes in the elementary school child. Starting from a stage in which prayer is simply a word associated with other words — such as *God* — that are essentially meaningless to the child, it comes to be conceived as a mental activity that is associated with a system of religious beliefs that are not shared by all children and peoples. Thus, the older child comes to view prayer more abstractly, more objectively, and in a more differentiated fashion than his or her younger counterparts. Similar trends were observed in the evolution of the contents, affects, and fantasies associated with prayer activity described next.

Content of Prayer

The age trends with respect to the content of thought can be briefly described. Among the younger children, the content of prayer was concerned primarily with the gratification of personal desires. With increasing age, however, there was a shift from asking for particular things for themselves to thanking God for things that they had already received. There was also an increasing concern among the older children with more humanitarian and altruistic requests such as for "peace" or for "the poor and the sick." At the same time, there was a decline in the tendency merely to recite standard prayers such as, "God bless Mother, Father." Thus, with increasing age, the content of prayer became more personal and individualized but at the same time less egoistic and self-centered.

Affects

With respect to the evolution of the affects associated with prayer, a clear-cut developmental trend was evident. Among young children, prayer was affectively neutral and was associated with certain fixed times such as before going to bed, at church, or prior to eating. This routinized and scheduled prayer activity gradually gave way among the older children to affect-laden prayer activity that arose spontaneously at any time in response to particular feelings. Thus, the older children prayed when they were worried, upset, lonely, or troubled as well as at bedtime or on Sundays. An interesting sidelight on this development was that negative feelings provided much more motivation for prayer than did positive feelings, an observation previously reported by Allport (1953) in another connection. At the same time, however, prayer activity itself seemed to be accompanied by pleasant emotions and the relaxation of tension.

Another aspect of the affective side of prayer development, revealed by the sentence, "When I see someone praying, I . . .," was what might be called increasing *empathy* with others. This was manifested in an increasing awareness among the older children of the fact that others pray for the same things and for the same reasons. Coupled with this increased empathy was what seemed to be an increased recognition of prayer as serving a constructive function in one's personal growth and character formation. Still another aspect of the affective side of prayer development was revealed by the questions dealing with what one is to do if prayers are or are not answered. The fact that prayers are not always answered distressed the younger children more than the older children and seemed to be associated with a wide variety of immature rage and frustration responses such as "Be mad at God" or "Cry" and "Scream." At the older age levels, responses to this question were more resigned and philosophical: "Thank Him, anyway" and "Keep praying for it." (The latter was the most frequent response among the older children.) Among the older children, there was also an increased recognition that one was personally responsible for the ends he or she desired and that God was a helper and not a magic genie who simply made one's wishes come true.

In short, the affects associated with the development of the prayer concept showed developmental trends similar to those observed with respect to the form and content of prayer. Emotional responses became more modulated and mature as prayer took on a personal affective meaning while becoming more impersonal in its objectives and goals.

Fantasy

The fantasy activity associated with the prayer concept was revealed by the questions that asked, "Where do prayers come from?" and "Where do prayers go?" Among the youngest children, prayers were thought to come from God, or from Heaven, or from Fairyland in the sky. At the same age level, there was a general tendency to regard prayers as self-propelled, in the sense that they were said to "fly," "float," or "jump" up to Heaven. Some children at this level said that God brought prayers to Heaven by magical means.

Among the somewhat older children (7–9 years), prayers were often said to come from people living in former times. Prayers were thus thought to have been made up by historical persons such as Moses, Abraham Lincoln, or the Pilgrims. Prayers were seen as having been passed on from these persons to us via books such as the Bible. At this stage, children seemed to believe that prayers were not self-propelled but were rather carried up to God by means of messengers or intermediaries. In some cases, God Himself was thought to descend to pick up the prayers.

After about the age of 9 or 10, prayers were no longer attributed to historical personages but were regarded as originating within the children themselves. The child was now the author of his or her own prayers. At the same time, children at this level said that prayers were heard by God directly and that there was no need for intermediaries or for means of propelling them to Heaven. Among the older children, God was considered as capable of attending to everyone's prayers at the same time, so that prayer was regarded as a form of direct communication.

Discussion

The foregoing pages have covered, in very condensed fashion, the results of our attempt to explore developmental changes in the form and content of children's prayers and with associated changes in affect and fantasy activity. What has been revealed is an apparently paradoxical development in which prayer and associated mental activities become both more objective and more subjective with increasing age. On one hand, with respect to the form of the prayer concept, the child's understanding becomes increasingly differentiated and abstract and increasingly divorced from personal elements.

At the same time, however, the content of prayer becomes increasingly personal and loses the stereotyped and rote quality that it has in early childhood. How to explain these apparently contradictory developments?

The solution to this problem probably lies in the consideration that in the young child, subjective and objective elements are not clearly differentiated. This lack of differentiation is revealed in the young child's consideration of subjective elements as objective and vice versa. Young children, for example, tended to think of prayers as *things* that needed to be propelled or carried to Heaven. At the same time, however, they also regarded animals as being able to talk, because dogs can bark, cats can meow, etc. Hence, these children tended to regard what was mental (prayer) as physical or thinglike and what was physical (dogs barking) as symbolic. Piaget (1929) has demonstrated this same lack of differentiation in another connection. Mental development thus involves the tendency to differentiate between objective and subjective elements, as was clearly shown in the evolution of prayer. Far from being in opposition to one another, objectivity and subjectivity are reciprocal, and every step in the direction of greater objectivity is also a step in the direction of greater subjectivity. In other words, it is impossible to learn what is independent of our own mental processes without at the same time learning something about those mental processes themselves. Hence, the reciprocal nature of objectivity and subjectivity. This development, it must be added, does not occur in a vacuum and is conditioned at every point by the interaction of maturing mental structures and the unending pressure of social norms.

It is interesting to compare these steps in the ontogenetic development of the prayer concept with those postulated by Hodge (1931) and Heiler (1932) for the historical and cultural evolution of prayer. According to these writers, prayer historically evolves in three stages: (1) primitive or tribal prayer, (2) ritual or rational prayer, and (3) universalistic or individualistic prayer. The first stage is seen as naive and spontaneous, largely motivated by man's inability to understand or control the forces of nature. It is thus mainly petitionary and wishful in content. Ritualistic prayer, in contrast, though still largely petitionary, is formalized, prescribed, stereotyped, and replete with sacred formulae and rites. The highest and final form of prayer, universalistic or individualistic, is seen as abstract — even to the point of being philosophical in tone. Its central theme is one of morality and goodness in which a contemplative relationship with an unchanging, ultimate deity provides the foundation for man's existence and life within an absolute system of ethical values. A somewhat similar evolutionary development for prayer has been proposed by Reik (1955), who described the development as moving from an emphasis on "My will be done" to "Thy will be done."

The parallel between these stages proposed to describe the historical and cultural evolution of prayer with the ontogenetic stages found in the development of the child's prayer concept is startling. But I am not proposing a recapitualtion theory of mental development such as that advocated by Hall (1908); rather I hold with Werner (1948) that if parallels exists between historical and ontogenetic sequences, then such parallels derive from the fact that development of the individual and of society are determined by common laws. On this assumption, the apparent parallel between the ontogenetic and phylogenetic stages in the evolution of prayer provides some external support for the validity of the sequence as described here.

Again, I would like to emphasize how, in the development of prayer as in the development of the child's conception of his or her religious denomination, three basic themes can be observed. At each stage of development, children construct a new concept of prayer that is neither entirely learned nor entirely spontaneous. Secondly, this process of construction is continuous, and the successive conceptions of prayer progressively approximate those held by adults. Finally, the concepts of prayer arrived at by children always reflect the interaction of mental activity and experience. At any stage of development, the child's conception of prayer represents the creative product of thought interacting with experience.

Perceptual Development in Children

INTRODUCTION

Jean Piaget is perhaps best known for his developmental theory of intelligence – adaptive thought and action. But Piaget has also elaborated a theory of perceptual development (Piaget, 1969) that complements and supports his work on the growth of intelligence. He assumes that perceptual reality, no less than conceptual reality, is constructed by the child as a consequence of his or her interactions with the environment. Like the construction of conceptual reality, the construction of perceptual reality is continuous throughout the whole life cycle. And finally, perceptual reality, no less than conceptual reality, is always an irreducible product of subject–object interaction. The development of perception, then, provides another illustration of the major themes of mental development from a constructionist perspective.

The construction of perceptual reality cannot of course be observed directly and must be inferred from children's performances on perceptual tasks. In elaborating his theory, Piaget limited himself almost exclusively to the use of visual illusions, and he did not try to demonstrate the theory's relevance for pictorial or symbolic stimuli. For more than a decade, my colleagues and I have been engaged in extending Piaget's theory to the perception of representational materials. The present chapter is an overview of some of our investigations and conclusions.

Before proceeding to describe that research, a brief résumé of Piaget's theory of perception is in order. In Piaget's view, the perception of the young child is *centered* in the sense that it is caught and held by one or another dominant aspect of the perceptual field. In each case, the dominant feature of the perceptual field is determined by organizational characteristics that the Gestalt psychologists described as continuity, closure, good form, and so on. A closed line drawing shows continuity of line, as well as closure of form, and hence is a more dominant figure than an unclosed or incomplete line drawing. These organizational characteristics of the stimulus are what Piaget calls *field effects*. The perception of the young child is thus centered, because it is almost completely dominated by the field effects.

As children grow older, however, their perception becomes progressively *decentered*, freed from its earlier domination by the field effects. This liberation is attained, thanks to the development of new perceptual abilities that Piaget speaks of as *perceptual regulations*. Perceptual regulations are semilogical processes that permit the child to mentally act upon the visual material. Perceptual regulations enable the child to reverse figure and ground, to coordinate parts and wholes, to explore systematically, to make comparisons at a distance, and to integrate the spatial and temporal features of a visual presentation. One part of our research has been to devise and to validate pictorial measures of these various regulations.

PICTORIAL MEASURES OF PERCEPTUAL REGULATIONS

Perceptual Reorganization

Perceptual reorganization has to do with the mental rearrangement of a perceived configuration. A wife, for example, who has her husband rearrange the furniture (or vice versa) usually has an idea in mind as to how things will look if they were otherwise put together. In experimental psychology, perceptual reorganization is often studied as figure- ground reversal and with the aid of ambiguous figures such as those shown in Figure 2.1. To the adult, figure— ground reversal (say from tree to duck in Drawing 2, Figure 2.1) appears to occur spontaneously and without conscious effort. It seems to be the result of the innate organizing principles described by Gestalt psychology rather than of the developmentally arrived-at regulations described by Piaget. Indeed, the Gestalt psychologists, Köhler and Wallach (1944), argued (on the basis of what today appears

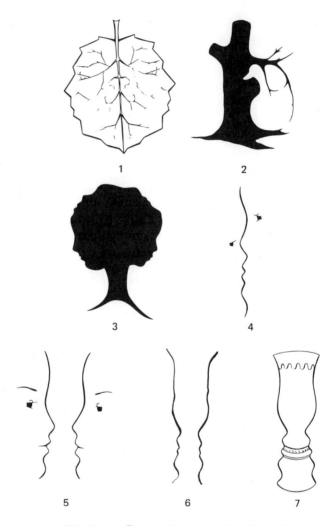

FIG. 2.1.   Picture Ambiguity Test (P.A.T.).

to be erroneous physiological assumptions about brain tissue) that figure–ground reversal should be more prominent in younger than in older children.

From a Piagetian standpoint, however, just the reverse prediction would be made. In Piaget's view, figure–ground reversal is mediated by logiclike processes that do not emerge until about the age of 6 or 7. To give a concrete example of how logic can help the child reverse figure and ground, consider Drawing 4 in Figure 2.1. If the center contour line is designated as C, the left area as LA, and the right area as RA, then figure (F) and ground (G) can be described as logical equations involving these terms. That is to say, when the left face is seen as figure and the right area is seen as ground, the following equations hold:

$$F = LA + C, \qquad G = RA - C$$

And when the right face is seen as figure and the left area is seen as ground, the following equations hold:

$$F = RA + C, \qquad G = LA - C$$

In effect, from a Piagetian point of view, figure–ground has to do with the various logical combinations of contours and areas.

It should be said, however, that the perceptual regulations that enable the child to recombine areas and contours are only "semi" logical and are not entirely identical with the operations of intelligence. This is true, because there are certain operations that can be performed mentally that are, nonetheless, impossible on the plane of perception. For example, on the plane of intelligence, the equation $F - LA = C$ is necessarily implied by the equation $F = C + LA$. On the perceptual plane, however, the equation $F - LA = C$ is not possible, because an individual cannot perceive a contour in isolation. Perceptually, a line is always a boundary and cannot be seen apart from the areas that it bounds. Regulations, therefore, do not generate a complete set of logical equations; and it is for this reason that Piaget speaks of them as being only partially "isomorphic" with the operations of intelligence.

To test the divergent predictions of the Gestalt and Piagetian conceptions of figure–ground reversal, we constructed a set of reversible figures – the Picture Ambiguity Test (P.A.T.) – (Figure 2.1) and administered them to 126 children from 4 to 11 years of age (Elkind & Scott, 1962). Results indicated that the ability to reverse figure and ground increased regularly with age. In addition, the ease with which children made figure–ground reversals was also related to the articulation of the figures. The more clearly drawn and recognizable the figures, the easier it was for children of all ages to reverse figure and ground. These findings support the view that percepts are constructions, that the process of constructing them is continuous, and that the resulting percept is a joint product of the perceptual activity of the subject *and* the nature of the stimulus.

One question is repeatedly raised when age data, such as those described above, are reported: What is the extent to which performance can be accelerated by training? Piaget's answer (to what he terms the "American question") is that there is an optimal time for the development of operations and regulations that cannot be hurried. Piaget also recognizes, however, that children may not always fully realize their abilities at the optimal time. Under these circumstances, he suggests that children will improve with training but that this improvement will always be relative to the child's level of mental development.

In order to test this hypothesis about the relation between development and learning, a second, complementary set of P.A.T. cards was drawn up for use in training investigations (Elkind, 1964). In one training study (Elkind, Koegler, & Go, 1962), children at three different age levels were first tested on one set of cards, then trained on the second set, and then retested on the first. The method of training involved a progressively more directive approach. After a spontaneous response to the cards, the children were first asked, "Do you see anything else besides a . . .?" If the children did not identify an additional figure, they were asked, "Do you see a face, a duck, a . . .?" If the children still did not see the reversed figure or figures, the other figure was masked so as to bring the reverse figure into prominence (Figure 2.2). The results of the study are given in Table 2.1. As this table indicates, all of the children improved with age; but younger children needed more cues and made less progress than the older children. These data support Piaget's contention that the effects of training are in part at least

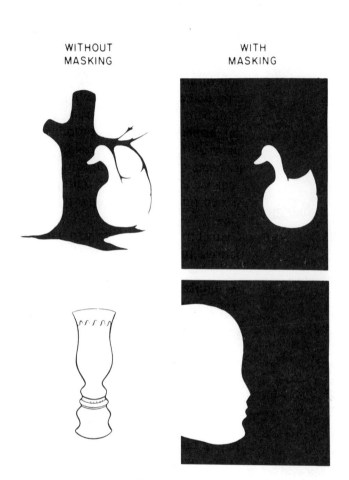

WITHOUT
MASKING

WITH
MASKING

FIG. 2.2.   Perceptual training figures.

determined by the child's overall level of mental development.

Perceptual Schematization

Perhaps the most well known tenet of Gestalt psychology is that "the whole is greater than the sum of its parts." A melody, for example, cannot be understood as the arithmetic sum of its parts, because the notes in relation to one another constitute a new whole that is primary and not reducible to the notes alone. The fact that a melody can be transposed into another key makes it clear that the whole is not dependent on specific parts. From a developmental point of view, however, the problem is whether the construction of wholes is due to the automatic workings of "built-in" Gestalt principles of organization or whether such wholes are mental constructions that must wait upon the development of perceptual regulations and mental operations.

Piaget's answer to this question is that there are at least two kinds of wholes. Undifferentiated or *figurative* wholes (such as your first impression of a painting) appear early in development and derive from the Gestalt principles of organization. With the development of perceptual regulations, however, children begin to perceive *operative* wholes (the overall impression of a painting after you have examined it in detail) that are the products of mental construction. The Gestalt psychologists do not distinguish between figurative and operative wholes

TABLE 2.1

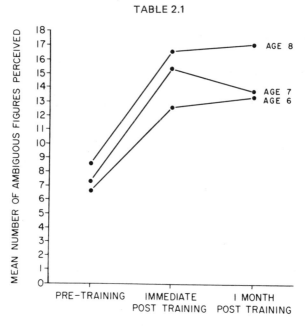

(because for them, all wholes are constituted in the same way), but this distinction is central to the Piagetian position. In a sense, a figurative whole can be regarded as a result of centering upon a dominant aspect of the visual field; whereas an operative whole can be regarded as the integration of all the various aspects of the stimulus configuration.

To assess the development of perceptual schematization (perception of operative wholes), a set of seven whole—part figures modeled after those used by Meili—Dworetzki (1956) was drawn up. This set, the Perceptual Integration Test (P.I.T.), is shown in Figure 2.3. The developmental assumption was that children who responded to either the parts or wholes in isolation would demonstrate a figurative approach, whereas children who saw wholes and parts in relation to one another would demonstrate an operative orientation. That is to say, for children to see a "man made out of fruit," they must recognize that one and the same form can have at least two different meanings. This requires a kind of logical multiplication of forms that is dependent on the development of regulations. For example, the perception of the indented circle in Figure 2.3, Drawing 2, as both a head and an apple is but one of the possible products of the multiplication of these two form classes. When the class of head forms is multiplied by the class of apple forms, at least four logical products are possible: the class of head forms that are also apple forms (HA), the class of head forms that are not

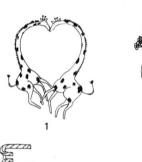

1

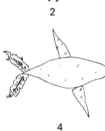

3

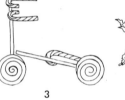

4

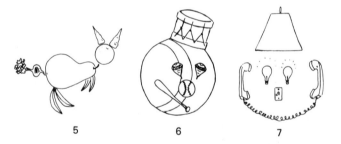

2

5

6

7

FIG. 2.3.   Picture Integration Test (P.I.T.).

apple forms (H$\overline{\text{A}}$), the class of apple forms that are not head forms (A$\overline{\text{H}}$), and the class of forms that are neither apple- nor head-shaped ($\overline{\text{NH}}$). All of these products are implicit, once the child says a "man made out of fruit."

The test of the hypothesis regarding the development from figurative to operative wholes was as follows: The P.I.T. cards were shown to 195 children from 4 to 9 years of age, who were instructed only to identify what they saw. The major results of the study (Elkind, Koegler, & Go, 1962) confirmed the prediction of the theory. There was a regular increase with age in the ability of children to perceive both parts and wholes. In addition, parts tended to be perceived earlier than wholes. And finally, part—whole integrations (operative wholes) were present in 75% of the children by the age of 9.

Although these findings seem to support the distinction between figurative and operative wholes suggested earlier, there are alternative explanations. Jerome Bruner (1964), for example, has suggested in connection with Piaget's (1950) conservation experiments that the age changes might reflect changes in representational ability rather than in intellectual or perceptual maturity. Applied to the data reported here, such a view suggests that the differences between the younger and older children lie primarily in the verbal formulae they have at their disposal. Older children would be in possession of the verbal formula, "X is made out of Y"; younger ones would not. If this view is correct, even young children should be able to see operative wholes, and their only difficulty would lie in their inability to express what they see.

In order to test the possibility that even young children see operative wholes but cannot express them, another study was carried out (Elkind, Anagnostopoulou, & Malone, 1970). Forty first-grade children were divided into two groups, depending on their scores on the P.I.T. They were then asked to reconstruct some part—whole figures from memory, to name some simple objects fabricated out of familiar materials, and to perform some logical tasks (class-inclusion tasks such as, "Are there more boys or more children in your class?"). The results showed that children who spontaneously reported operative wholes on the pretest were significantly more likely to reconstruct operative wholes from memory, to use the formula, "X is made out of Y," and to perform logical operations on classes than were children who reported only figurative wholes on the pretest. Because children who did not report operative wholes were also unable to reconstruct them from memory, the hypothesis that young children actually see operative wholes but merely do not report them was not substantiated.

Before closing this section on schematization, a study deriving from some qualitative observations of children's performance on the P.I.T. should be reported. A rather strange type of response was sometimes noted among the 5- and 6-year-old children. Occasionally a child of this age would say, "Some fruit. No, I mean a man." Then, if the examiner asked the child to name the fruit, the child would say, "No fruit, just a man." It seemed as if these children saw the parts and the whole in alternation rather than simultaneously. One interpretation of this observation is that perceptual regulations make a temporal contribution and literally "speed up" the perceptual process when they appear developmentally. In older children and adults, perhaps, the speed of perceptual integration may mask the actual constructive process and give the impression that operative wholes are arrived at by a simple "reading" of the perceptual configuration.

To assess this temporal dimension to schematization, we carried out a tachistoscopic investigation (Whiteside, Elkind, & Golbeck, 1976). The P.I.T. figures were shown to 128 children from 3 to 12 years of age. Four stimulus durations were used — .1, 1.0, 5.0, and 10.0 seconds. Each subject saw four different figures at four different durations. The proportion of total responses that were operative wholes for the four durations and the four age groups is given in Table 2.2. There was a significant difference between the age groups in the proportions of operative wholes reported and also a significant difference in the number of operative wholes given at the different duration intervals. At each age level, the proportion of operative wholes was greater for the longer delay intervals than for the shorter ones. For the older children, however, a relatively high proportion of operative wholes was given at even relatively short durations. These data support the observation that growth in perceptual

TABLE 2.2

PROPORTION OF INTEGRATED RESPONSES AS
A FUNCTION OF AGE AND EXPCSURE DURATION

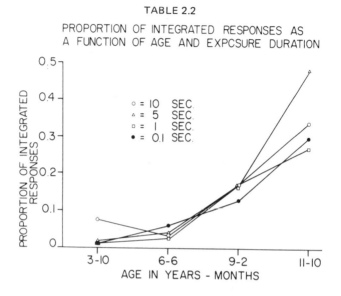

regulations involves not only a higher order integration of the perceptual material but also a more rapid
integration of the stimulus information.

Perceptual Exploration

Perhaps the most frequently employed perceptual
regulation has to do with the scanning or systematic
exploration of the visual field. Trying to find your
car in the airport parking lot after being away for a
few days (particularly if you haven't noted down
where you left it) is a familiar kind of perceptual
exploration. According to Gestalt psychology, such
exploration should follow the path of good Gestalts
and of "least effort." (For example, the rows made
by the cars in the parking lot are a "good form,"
and looking up and down the rows is less effortful

than looking back and forth between several rows at a time.) From a developmental point of view, however, regulations should enable older children to overcome the constraints of good form and of least effort and permit them, should they so desire, to explore the field as they choose.

To test the development of children's perceptual exploration abilities, we constructed another pictorial measure, the Picture Exploration Test (P.E.T.) (Figure 2.4). The test consists of 2 cards upon which 15 pictures of familiar objects (lamp, fish, chair, etc.) were pasted. On one card, the *disordered array* card, the pictures were pasted in an irregular fashion, so that they did not suggest rows, columns, or figures of any kind. On the other card, the *ordered array* card, the pictures were pasted in a triangular pattern. For control purposes, a second set of ordered and disordered array cards was constructed with the same pictures, except that the pictures used in the disordered array card were placed in an ordered array and vice versa.

The P.E.T. was administered to 85 children from 5 to 8 years of age. Each child was shown both an ordered and disordered array card and was asked to name every picture on each card. Results of the study (Elkind & Weiss, 1967) yielded quite different results for the two cards. On the disordered array card, young children made errors of commission (they named some figures twice) and of omission (they failed to name some figures at all). Older children made no such errors and named all of the figures correctly. In naming the figures, they tended to start at the top left-hand corner and to name the figures from left to right

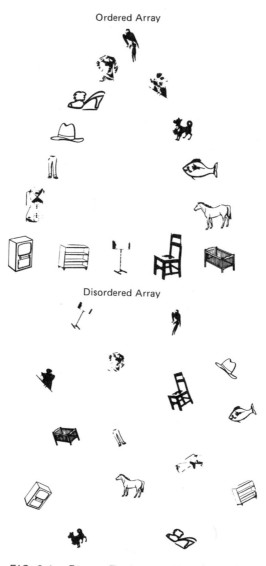

FIG. 2.4   Picture Exploration Test (P.E.T.).

and from top to bottom. The young children showed no such systematic pattern in the order in which they named the figures.

A rather different set of findings was obtained with the ordered, triangular array card. The shape formed a "good" Gestalt, and it was expected that young children would not have as much trouble naming the figures in this array as they did on the disordered one. This was indeed the case, and even the young children made no errors of omission or commission. There were, in fact, no differences between the various age groups in their error scores on the triangular array. There was, however, an interesting age difference in the pattern of exploration employed at different age levels that reveals an important facet of perceptual growth.

As expected, the 5-year-olds read the figures around the triangle, starting at the top. This was also the pattern employed by the 8-year-olds. But many of the 6- and 7-year-old youngsters (first and second graders) read the triangle from left to right and from top to bottom. This was far from the Gestalt path of least effort as far as visual movement was concerned. Our interpretation of this finding was that the first- and second-grade children were just beginning to learn to read and that they were spontaneously practicing the left-to-right, top-to-bottom "swing" required in reading. By the time most children reach third grade, the left-to-right swing is mastered and no longer needs to be practiced on any material presented. This hypothesis was supported by the results of Kugelmass and Lieblich (1970), who replicated the study in Israel. They found that their first- and second-grade children also read the triangle across, but from right to left — the direction employed in reading Hebrew.

These findings in the ordered-array experiment point up a significant feature in the relation between the Gestalt field effects and perceptual regulations. The field effects described by Gestalt psychology — figure–ground, good form, continuity, and so on — appear to be basic organizing principles that continue to operate throughout the life span. The development of perceptual regulations provide older children and adults alternatives to the field-effect modes of organization. Sometimes these alternative modes of organization become as automatic as the regulations themselves in some stimulus contexts. The part–whole organizations described earlier and the left-to-right swing employed on the P.I.T. reflected these automatized regulations. Sometimes, however, the stimulus materials allow for alternative organizations — either Gestalt or regulational — as in the case of the triangular array. Under these conditions, comparable perceptual performances may conceal quite different perceptual competencies. Both kindergarten and third-grade children read the triangular array around the form. But the older children could read the array from left to right if they chose or were asked to do so; the kindergarten children could not. In situations where alternative modes of organization are possible, the possession of regulations gives older children alternatives not available to younger children.

Perceptual Transport

One of the most basic regulations has to do with making perceptual comparisons across a distance, an activity Piaget calls *perceptual transport.* Piaget studied the development of perceptual transport by having subjects compare vertical lines, of equal and unequal lengths, at different distances. He found that successful size judgments were more frequent with increasing age and that older children were more successful than younger children in making size judgments across large spatial distances.

Piaget attributes his findings to the interaction of several different processes, which make their appearance gradually in the course of development. In his view, the age effects are due to the fact that the youngest children center upon one of the comparison stimuli and overestimate its size in relation to the other. As children grow older, the tendency to center upon, and hence to overestimate, one or another of the stimuli diminishes, as does the overall number of errors.

Piaget attributes the distance effects to reciprocal transport, a regulation that only the older children are capable of employing. To illustrate Piaget's notion of reciprocal transport, let the comparison stimuli of a transport problem be labeled A and B. Comparisons of A with B ($A \rightarrow B$) or of B with A ($B \leftarrow A$) are instances of *unilateral transport.* A *reciprocal transport* would be a comparison of A with B and of B with A ($A \rightleftarrows B$). Unilateral transport, like centering, tends to introduce errors of over- and underestimation. In addition, reciprocal transport becomes more difficult as distance between the comparison stimuli increases. Consequently, at large separation distances, unilateral transport is more frequent, and size judgment errors are more frequent as well.

In order to assess the development of perceptual transport with more pictorial materials, we constructed 12 pairs of geometric figures. Both members of a pair had the same form, but one was slightly larger than the other. The 12 pairs of geometric figures were called the Picture Uniformity Test (P.U.T.) (Figure 2.5). Each pair of geometric figures was photographed at three different separation distances (2.54 cm, 12.70 cm, and 22.86 cm) and with the standard (larger figure) in both the right and left position at each separation distance. Taking into account the three distances and the two positions for each member of the pair, there were 72 possible examples of each pair. These examples were randomly divided into 2 sets of 36 problems that made up the actual items of the test.

One hundred and twenty children (24 at each age level from 5 to 9) were tested on one of the two sets of 36 problems making up the P.U.T. The child's task was merely to say for each pair of geometric figures which of the two figures was the largest. Results (Farkas & Elkind, 1974) showed that success in making size comparisons at a distance (1) increased significantly with age; (2) decreased significantly as distance increased; (3) was

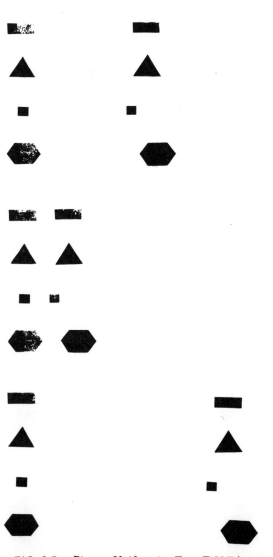

FIG. 2.5   Picture Uniformity Test (P.U.T.).

significantly better when the standard (larger) figure was on the left than when it was on the right; and (4) increased with age when the standard was on the right.

These results are in keeping with Piaget's notions regarding centering and reciprocal transport. In addition, the position effects reinforce our P.E.T. findings that children have a strong tendency to explore from left to right. It is this position preference, or so it seemed to us, that accounted for the strong position effects in the study. When the standard was on the left, the young children tended to center upon it and to overestimate its size. This enhanced their chances of making a correct size discrimination. When the smaller figure was on the left, however, the overestimation of the left figure worked in the other direction and made a correct size discrimination more difficult. With increased age, and the ability to decenter, this position effect would according to the theory diminish. This is in fact what occurred. The complexity of the regulations and of their interactions underlying even apparently simple size judgments are well illustrated by these findings.

Expectation

The last regulation for which we have developed pictorial measures is what Piaget calls *anticipation* in French, but that in English is best translated here as *expectation.* On the basis of Piaget's theory, one might look for the appearance of two types of perceptual expectation in children. Young children, who lack the ability to coordinate perceptual regulations, might display a *figurative expectation*, defined as a focusing to such an extent on the temporal characteristics of a stimulus series that they do not correctly perceive its individual members. For example, a child who is so concerned with the movement and sound of the train going by that he does not attend to which car is the engine, which the freight, and which the caboose, illustrates a figurative expectation. Older children, who are able to coordinate perceptual regulations, work under an *operative expectation*, in which the coordination of lower order regulations enables them to move on from temporal features and to arrive at a true perception of the series as a whole as well as of its individual members. The child who appreciates not only the succession of cars in a train but also that the engine came first and the caboose last provides an example of an operative expectation.

To investigate the development from figurative to operative expectation, we employed a "violation of expectation" procedure. An expectation is built up in the child by the presentation of a series of stimuli and is violated by the presentation of a critical figure that is not in keeping with the series pattern. To illustrate, consider a series of line drawings of boys and girls in a particular sequence (i.e., boy, girl, boy, girl, and so on) that contains, at a late point in the series, two pictures of boys in succession (a violation of expectation). Suppose now that a child is shown this series. If — on presentation of the second boy picture — he or she responds "girl," we would infer that the child demonstrated *temporal centering* (exclusive focus on the temporal pattern); and we would infer that he or she had a figurative expectation. If in contrast the child said "boy" to the critical figure, we would say that he or she showed *temporal decentering* (focus upon individual members of the temporal pattern as well as upon the pattern as a whole), and we would infer that the child possessed an operative expectation.

The above example suggests that whether or not the child focuses upon the temporal features of the series will depend on several different factors. One of these is his or her age — a rough gauge of his or her level of perceptual development. Another is the relative strength (in Gestalt terms of continuity, closure, etc.) of the pattern vis-à-vis the critical (violation of expectation) figure. In the foregoing illustration, for example, suppose that the boy—girl differences in the drawings of the series were recognizable but not clear-cut and that the critical figure was clearly and unmistakably a boy. Under these circumstances, we might expect that temporal centering would be weaker than when the reverse situation (clearly articulated series figures and an ambiguous critical figure) obtained.

On the stimulus side, therefore, temporal centering would seem to be a joint function of the Gestalt features of the pattern vis-à-vis those of the critical, violation of expectation figure. To assess the effects of this stimulus determinant of temporal decentering, four series of stimuli and four critical figures were employed. Two of the series were arranged to present a strong temporal pattern, and two were arranged to present a weak one. Likewise, two of the critical figures were clearly articulated (providing strong Gestalt figures), and two were ambiguous (providing weak Gestalt figures). These levels of ambiguity were determined by showing the critical figures in isolation to pilot groups of children. Four combinations of weak/strong temporal patterns and weak/strong critical figures were thus possible. These four patterns were: strong temporal pattern, strong critical figure (SS); strong temporal pattern, weak critical figure (SW); weak temporal pattern, strong critical figure (WS); and weak temporal pattern, weak critical figure (WW). The four sets of stimuli were called the Picture Opposition Test (P.O.T.) (Figure 2.6).

All four P.O.T. series were shown to 60 children (10 boys and 10 girls at the 4-, 6-, and 8-year levels) by means of slides and a rear-view projection screen. Results (Meyer & Elkind, 1975) showed that there was a significant decrease with age in temporal centering (figurative expectation) and that the extent of temporal centering was directly related to Gestalt characteristics of the series. Temporal centering was greatest to the SW pattern and least to the WS pattern. But the extent of temporal centering to the SW pattern decreased with age. This latter finding might be taken as an index of the emergence of temporal decentration and operative expectancy. Other evidence of operative expectancy was the correlation of .40 between

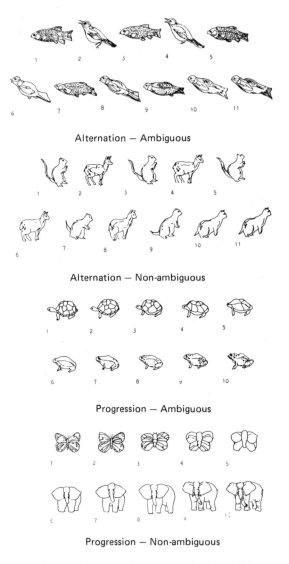

Alternation — Ambiguous

Alternation — Non-ambiguous

Progression — Ambiguous

Progression — Non-ambiguous

FIG. 2.6   Picture Opposition Test (P.O.T.).

subjects' perception of systematic change in the animal figures and temporal decentration. These data support the view that the child's reaction to the temporal dimensions of perceptual configuration follows the same developmental course as his or her reactions to their spatial characteristics.

Perceptual Development and Reading

Our work on perceptual regulations supports Piaget's view that perceptual reality, like conceptual reality, is not preformed or learned but rather is constructed with the aid of semilogical regulations. It is important to emphasize, however, that the development of regulations and the resulting figure— ground reversal, schematization, and so on are constructed by most children on their own and without specific tutelage. This happens, because such constructions are necessary to survival; the child is forced to construct them as he or she interacts with the physical world. The same is true for the many "conservation" concepts that, as Piaget (1950) has demonstrated, develop during the elementary school years.

It is important to stress the spontaneous development of these perceptual skills, because many attempts to "apply" Piaget have been efforts to teach children mental constructions that they will acquire on their own. There is a danger that the same might be done with the regulational constructions described here. But aside from training studies — such as those described in this article —

designed to reveal processes, it makes little sense to teach children what they will learn on their own, anyway. Piaget has provided us not with new *contents* to teach children but rather with new *tools* for looking at the skills and contents that children do not learn on their own and that they need instruction to acquire. Put differently, Piaget has provided us not with a new curriculum but rather with new tools for curriculum analysis.

In applying our work to educational issues, therefore, we have tried to look at skills children need to acquire in terms of the regulations that these skills seem to presuppose. Beginning reading is a case in point; and we might ask, "What regulations must a child possess in order to acquire and utilize decoding or phonic skills?" To answer that question, we must begin with the basic units of reading — namely, letters and sounds. From a Piagetian standpoint, these units are constructions rather than preformed or merely learned "units." What regulations are required for their construction?

In standard English, a single letter, say t, can be represented in several different ways. It can be presented as lower case or upper case and in script or roman. Moreover, when used in a word, one and the same letter can be associatedw with different sounds (t in to and in $t$he), and one and the same sound can be represented by different letters (sun, son). In constructing letters as phonic units, therefore, the child is confronted with problems analogous to those he or she meets in dealing with figure—ground reversal and schematization of part and whole.

To make this analogy concrete, recall that the child has to multiply contours and areas in order to produce all the combinations of figure and ground that are possible in a reverse/profile configuration. It seems reasonable to propose that a similar regulational system is required by a child in order to read an o as $\bar{o}$ in flow and as $\grave{o}$ in soft. In a sense, the child must multiply letters and sounds to arrive at the various combinations that occur in English phonics. Thus if we multiply any letter l by any sound s, we would get $s \times l =$ the combination of the letter and the sound (sl), the sound without the letter ($s\bar{l}$), the letter without the sound ($\bar{s}l$), and neither the letter nor the sound ($\bar{s}\bar{l}$). If we multiply across all letters and letter combinations (morphemes) and all sounds and sound blends (phonemes) that are found in standard English, we could generate all the combinations that occur in English phonics.

From this standpoint, therefore, beginning reading — the acquisition of phonic skills — would seem to involve among other things the development of perceptual regulations. To test this hypothesis, we carried out a number of different studies relating the development of perceptual regulations to reading achievement. In the first, descriptive study (Elkind, Horn, & Schneider, 1965), 180 elementary school children were given a battery of tests including (1) the P.A.T. and P.I.T.; (2) some verbal decentering tasks such as run on sentences (THEBOYRANAWAY) and reading words upside down; and (3) a set of standard reading achievement measures. Factor analysis of the data showed that all the tests loaded heavily on a common factor. That is to say, a common ability appeared to underly successful performance on both the perceptual and the reading tests. Presumably, the common underlying ability had to do with decentering. This initial finding supported the theoretical analyses of the relation between reading and perceptual decentration.

It might be argued however, that the factor analytic results were spurious, because there was no control for intelligence. Perhaps the real underlying factor in all the tests was mental brightness. To test this hypothesis, we carried out another training study with the two sets of P.A.T. cards described earlier. The subjects were 60 children, 30 of whom were at grade level or better in reading achievement and 30 of whom were either 1 or 2 years behind in their reading and were receiving remedial reading instruction. The children were chosen from the total school population and were matched by age, sex, and a nonverbal measure of IQ (the Otis alpha). The testing, training, and re-training procedures were exactly the same as those employed in the training study described earlier.

The results of the study are shown in Tables 2.3 and 2.4 (Elkind, Larson, & Van Doorninck, 1965). As shown in Table 2.3, the slow readers were significantly behind the average readers on the P.A.T. pretest. In addition, both the slow and average readers made significant improvement as a result of training, but the average group remained significantly ahead of the slow group. Finally, as Table 4 indicates, the slow readers required significantly more learning trials than did the average readers. In general, these findings support the hypothesis that perceptual regulations, and not just general intelligence, are involved in beginning reading.

To follow up these findings, we carried out a more extensive training study in a natural laboratory, the classroom (Elkind & Deblinger, 1969). Two groups of second-grade, inner-city children were matched for reading achievement and perceptual ability as assessed by the P.I.T. and P.A.T. The experimental group was trained by the author with a series of nonverbal perceptual exercises for ½ hour three times a week for a period of 15 weeks. The control group met with the author for a comparable amount of time but was trained with a commercial reading program (the *Bank Street readers*). Results showed that the experimental group made significantly greater improvement on word form and recognition than did the control group. Although the control group

TABLE 2.3

Pre- and Posttraining Mean Scores and Differences for
Two Reading Groups and Two Age Levels

Reading group	N	Age level	Pretraining	Posttraining	d
Slow	15	Younger	8.67	15.30	6.46*
	15	Older	9.67	15.07	5.40*
Average	15	Younger	11.67	19.27	7.80*
	15	Older	13.33	18.87	5.47*

*$p < .01$.

TABLE 2.4
Learning Score Means and Differences for Two Age
Levels and Two Reading Groups

| Age group | Reading group | | d |
	Slow	Average	
Younger	17.13	11.80	5.33*
Older	15.13	10.53	4.60*
Total	16.13	11.16	4.97*

*$p < .01$.

spent more time than the experimental group on comprehension exercises, the two groups were not significantly different on this measure.

All of these studies support the notion that reading English, far from being a simple matter of discriminating letters and associating sounds, involves complex mental processes from the very start. This hypothesis can also be demonstrated by showing that in languages where the logical difficulties are absent, children can read with facility at an early age. This happens with phonetic languages like Japanese. A recent survey of reading disabilities in Japan (Makita, 1969) indicates their incidence is 0.98%, or 10 times lower than those in Western countries. Written Japanese consists of three varieties of script — two Kana (phonetic) scripts, each of which consists of 48 phonetic figures, and Kanji, which consists of 1,850 ideographs. There is a central difference between the Kana scripts and English. In Kana, the figures are always sounded in the same way; and hence the scripts, with which children learn Japanese, present children with more complex discrimination tasks than English letters but with many fewer logical difficulties. The low incidence of reading disabilities among Japanese children probably results from this fact. As Makita (1969) says:

> Theories which ascribe the etiology of reading disability to local cerebral abnormalities, to laterality conflict, or to emotional pressure may be valid for some instances; but the specificity of the used language, the very object of reading behavior, is the most potent contributing factor in the formation of reading disability. Reading disability, then, is more of a philological than a neuropsychiatric problem [p. 249].

Of course in teaching children English, removing the logical problems is not very helpful, because the child will have to deal with them eventually. This may be why i.t.a. (Downing, 1971), the international teaching alphabet (44 characters, each of which is associated with a single English phoneme), has not been very successful. The situation has a private analogy. When the author's son Bobby was 4 years old, he discovered that he could tell time by reading the digital clock in his parents' bedroom. The digital clock removes the logical difficulty of telling time from a regular clock face, where one and the same figure can stand for both 1 hour and for 5 minutes. But Bobby's success in reading the digital clock did not help him very much in telling time from a standard watch, a skill it took him several additional years to acquire.

It should be said that in stressing the importance of logical abilities in initial reading, the writer in no way means to imply that such abilities are all that is required for a child to begin reading. Our recent work (Briggs & Elkind, 1973, 1977) with early readers (children who read before they enter kindergarten) suggests that many factors — including motivation, an environment rich in language experiences, and interested adults who model and reward reading behavior — are all involved. What *is* being argued here is that perceptual regulations are a necessary, although not a sufficient, condition for successful beginning reading. One implication of this conclusion is that formal instruction in reading (i.e., phonics training) might be delayed with profit until the majority of children can be expected to have perceptual regulations, namely, at age 6 to 7. Prior to that, being read to, exposure to new words, and learning to identify and print letters are all valuable preparations for formal instruction in reading. On the other hand, no roadblock should be put in the way of those young children (about 1 in a 100) who show a spontaneous interest in reading.

This chapter has summarized some of our research growing out of Piaget's theory of perceptual development. In general, our findings support Piaget's view that perception as well as intelligence are neither entirely inborn nor entirely innate but are rather progressively *constructed* through the gradual development of perceptual regulations. The chapter has also attempted to demonstrate the applicability of Piaget's theory to practical issues by summarizing some research growing out of an analysis of beginning reading. Results support the analysis and suggest that beginning reading requires the logiclike process made possible by perceptual regulations. In closing, it is necessary to emphasize once again that Piaget's work on perception has provided us not with a new perceptual curriculum but rather with new and powerful tools for the analysis of many different perceptual skills and performances.

Egocentrism 3

THE PROBLEM OF EGOCENTRISM

Mental development can be described in different ways and from different perspectives. In the discussion of religious development, we focused primarily upon the content changes and demonstrated how children's conceptions of their religious denomination and of prayer progressively approximated that of adults. The discussion of perceptual development, in contrast, was much more concerned with mental processes and tried to show how the perceptual regulations of young children develop into those of older children and adults.

In this chapter we look at mental development from still a third perspective, namely, that of egocentrism. Egocentrism, in general, has to do with the limitations of children's developing cognitive abilities rather than with their accomplishments. Constructing and reconstructing the world is a complex endeavor that takes time and effort and that does not happen all at once. When we deal with egocentrism, then, we emphasize the differences rather than the similarities between child and adult thinking.

In discussing egocentrism, we can look at cognitive development as involving several cognitive tasks. These tasks include: (1) the differentiation between transient and abiding facets of reality; (2) the differentiation between objective and subjective aspects of reality; and (3) the differentiation between universal and particular facets of reality. At each stage of development, these tasks have a different content and structure, but the same types of differentiation must be made. A child's failure at any given level of development to make one or all of these differentiations is evidence of egocentrism.

It should be clear, therefore, that egocentrism as it is used here is not a pejorative term but rather a developmental one. It suggests that the child has not yet made some differentiations that he or she will in fact eventually make. Perhaps an illustration will help. One of the cognitive tasks of the infant is to distinguish between transient sights and sounds and abiding objects. Young infants often behave as if an object no longer existed when it is out of sight and attend to a transient sight (such as a pattern of light) as if it were an abiding part of their world. To call such behavior egocentric is merely to indicate that the infant shows a particular lack of differentiation between self and world.

Before describing the stages of development from the standpoint of egocentrism, a couple of other remarks should be made. First, egocentric behavior provides still another kind of evidence for the hypotheses with which we began. A child's failure to differentiate between self and world results in constructions of reality that have the characteristics of the other constructions we have already discussed; they are genuine constructions, they change in the course of development, and they are irreducible products of subject—object interaction.

Egocentric behavior, however, has another value as well. It provides a nice bridge between discussions of cognition and discussions of affect, of feeling, and motivation. This is true, because the child's egocentric constructions often run afoul of adult realities and produce conflict. At least some parent—child dissension, for example, can be attributed to conflicting realities rather than to conflicting motives and desires. Although we cannot go into this matter in great detail, some hints of the interpersonal difficulties produced by the child's egocentric behavior are given along the way.

One last word before we turn to the discussion of egocentrism proper. It is useful to see each stage of development described by Piaget as having to do with the construction of a particular facet of the self-concept (see Table 3.1). The failures of differentiation at any given level of development can then be seen in the context of the child's self-concept as well as in the context of the surrounding world.

TABLE 3.1

Development of the Self and Associated Cognitive Constructions

Age period	Mental operations, Major achievements	Transient vs. abiding	Objective vs. subjective	Universal vs. particular
0–2 years *The Sensorimotor Self* (self as object)	1. Sensorimotor coordinations 2. Construction of a world of permanent objects	Distinguish between sounds, sights, etc. that are transient from those that are abiding.	Distinguish between disappearance caused by the object's movements and those brought about by the subject's own movements.	Distinguish between human faces in general and mother's face in particular.
2–6 years *The Symbolic Self* (self as symbol creator and user)	1. Preoperations and the symbolic function 2. Construction of a system of representations of the object world	Distinguish between symbols that are temporary designations ("leader," etc.) and permanent designations (names, religious affiliations, and so on).	Distinguish between symbols the child has created and those that are collective in origin.	Distinguish between use of symbols for the one and for the many ("Daddy" for one man only).

Age / Stage	Cognitive features			
6–11 years *The Lawful Self* (self as rule maker and follower)	1. Concrete operations 2. Construction of rules governing objects and representations	Distinguish rules made up for the moment (games, etc.) and more abiding rules such as those related to cheating, lying, etc.	Distinguish between rules the child assumes are operative and those that are actually in play.	Distinguish between rules and exceptions to them (language rules, game rules, as they apply to handicapped children, etc.).
11–15 *The Reflective Self* (self as theory builder and tester)	1. Formal operations 2. Construction of ideals, theories	Distinguish between momentary thoughts and theories and those that are abiding (Momentary thoughts sometimes assumed to be abiding need to be warded off.)	Distinguish between ideas held by the self and ideas held by others (imaginary audience constructions).	Distinguish between ideas unique to the self and those that are universal to mankind (personal fable).

INFANCY

In Piagetian psychology, the infancy period is called the *sensorimotor* period and lasts from birth till about 2 years. The primary cognitive task of the young infant is to construct a world of permanent objects and a conception of himself or herself as an object. This construction entails a complex series of coordinations of such behavior patterns as looking–touching, and hearing.

The course of this construction can be described in terms of the three types of differentiation described earlier. With respect to the transient and the abiding, the infant has to learn many complex skills. For example, during the first months of life an infant will not search for an object it has seen hidden. Toward the end of the 1st year, a child will begin to search for hidden objects but has trouble with displacement. If a baby sees an object hidden first in one place and then another, he or she will continue to search for it in the first place. Only toward the end of the 2nd year are infants able to distinguish between transient and permanent placements of objects.

The differentiation between the subjective and the objective also comes about gradually. For example, the young infant sucks on anything and everything that touches its mouth. In effect, he or she attempts to transform everything into a nipple or at least into something that can be sucked. Eventually, the infant begins to distinguish between those objects such as a thumb that are worthy of being sucked and those objects, such as the tail-end of a bottle, that are not. The infant begins to discriminate between how he or she would like the world to be and how it really is. Many other examples of the subject/object discrimination during infancy could be given, but perhaps this one will suffice to make the point.

Finally, the differentiation between the universal and the particular can also be seen during the infancy period. During the first few months of life, an infant will usually smile and giggle up at any human face that smiles first or in return. But by the end of the 1st year of life and into the 2nd, the infant becomes more discriminating. Some infants show "stranger anxiety" and manifest a fear of strange faces. So, by the end of the 1st year most infants have a pretty good differentiation between parent and/or caregiver faces and human faces in general.

It should be said, too, that at this stage the child also begins to show a beginning sense of self as object. By the end of the 1st year, most infants have a pretty good sense of their body parts and how they operate. In addition, stranger anxiety and a reticence to crawl downstairs suggest that the child also has a sense of an object self that can be hurt or taken away. The sense of self as a permanent object among other objects is a great cognitive advance for the infant but brings with it new anxieties and fears.

EARLY CHILDHOOD

The age period from about the age of 2 to 6 has been called by Piaget *the preoperational period*. As we have just seen, the child moves into this period having constructed a world of permanent objects and with a sense of himself or herself as still another object situated in the world. Toward the end of the 2nd year of life the child acquires a new set of mental abilities that Piaget, following a European psychological tradition, calls the *symbolic function*. What the symbolic function enables young children to do is to represent, or to symbolize, the world of objects that they created during the sensorimotor period.

It has to be emphasized that the symbolic function entails much more than the acquisition of language. At this stage, children not only learn words to represent their experience; they also engage in symbolic play (a stone is a turtle, a chair is a car, and so on) and report their first dreams and nightmares. They can also engage in *deferred imitation*, which involves watching an activity at one time and imitating it at a much later time. For example, a child who has come home from the doctor's office may try to put his or her souvenir tongue depressor into the mouth of an unwilling younger sibling.

In addition to being able to symbolize the world and to think in images, the symbolic function also enables the child to symbolize himself or herself. The child learns not only his or her name but also pronouns of possession such as *my* and *mine* and of assertion such as *I* and *me*. At this stage, then, the child begins to construct what might be called a *representational* or *symbolic self* made up of all the representations the child believes pertain to himself or herself. The egocentrism of this period pertains not only to representations of the world but also to representations of the self.

First of all, let us look at the matter of transient and abiding representations. Possession, for example, is a representational relationship. And it is in the area of possession that the young child's failure to distinguish between the transient and the abiding is most apparent. Consider the matter of sharing — a behavior that children in the United States — but not in Europe — are supposed to acquire in early childhood. But most parents and teachers find that the averaage preschooler is rather unwilling to share his or her possessions.

Why should this be so? Recall that possession is a representational relationship — a toy is a child's by virtue of one representative activity, namely, labeling. But play is also a representative activity. For a young child, playing with a toy also signifies ownership of the toy. If another child plays with his or her toy, this signifies ownership that the young child, understandably, does not want to relinguish. One reason for a young child's unwillingness to share his or her toys, therefore, is a failure to differentiate between transient and abiding representations of ownership. The young child does not differentiate between transient ownership conferred by use and abiding ownership conferred by entitlement or ownership according to law.

As an aside, a practical suggestion for teaching young children to share derives from this understanding about their egocentric conception of sharing. What the child is concerned about is entitlement, not use. To the child, use signifies entitlement. But if a child's name is written on a card and the card is then taped to the toy in question, most children will be willing to share. To a child, a written symbol is a more potent sign of entitlement than use. He or she will be willing to let other children use personal toys, so long as those toys bear a written symbol of the owner's entitlement.

We can turn now to the matter of differentiation between the subjective and the objective at the preschool level. The young child's failure to differentiate the subjective from the objective is prominent in a number of representational areas. Young children, for example, sometimes create their own words. These new words are often quite descriptive and suggest original ways of cutting up, or conceptualizing, the world. One child, to illustrate, called a mustache a "mouthbrow," and another called her father's brief case a "workpurse." In using these terms, however, children don't bother to define them. They assume that these words are the same as those of the collective vocabulary. In this sense, they fail to distinguish between subjective designations and those that are socially shared.

The young child's failure to distinguish between objective and subjective designations can be observed in other facets of his or her behavior. For example, children tend to think that names are part of things, that "moon," say, is a sort of physical property of the orb that shines in the sky at night. Children also believe that anything that has a name or representation must be tangible. Such psychic phenomena as dreams and toothaches are regarded as physical and as capable of being shared or experienced by more than one person. "Can't you feel how bad my tooth hurts?", a child at this stage once asked me.

In addition to their difficulties with the objective and the subjective, young children also have trouble with symbolic designations of the one and of the many. Language itself is ambiguous in this regard, because a single word such as *dog, car, house,* etc. can be used to designate a unique individual or a class of things. We say, "If that dog digs another hole in my lawn, I will call the dog catcher"; but we also say, "The dog is man's best friend." Likewise, we say, "The car won't start"; but also, "The car has changed civilization." Clearly, whether we mean *dog* or *car* in an individual or collective sense can only be determined by the context of the sentence.

The correct understanding and use of terms that can refer both to an individual and to a class require mental abilities that the preschool child has yet to obtain. At this stage a child does not yet have a clear conception of a class, i.e., elements that are all alike in one way but different in others. When young children are asked to group things, such as colored plastic, geometric forms, they do not group according to form or color. Rather they try to construct a figure such as a house wherein the particular elements form a larger, pictorial whole.

Perhaps the most familiar example of the young child's difficulty with the one and the many is his or her use of the terms "Daddy" and "Mommy." Many mothers tell stories about walking with their preschool children, who proceed to call many strange men "Daddy." In such instances, the child uses the term *Daddy* to stand for any particular man who may resemble his or her Daddy. The child's usage of the term is somewhere between the generic concept of man and the individual concept of a particular man. A similar phenomenon occurs when the preschool child calls his or her female nursery teacher "Mommy."

The child's egocentric confusions with regard to symbols can have affective consequences. Mainly this occurs because parents misinterpret the child's behavior. What happens is that when parents do not understand a child's behavior, they attribute bad motives to it. When, to illustrate, a child is reluctant to share — for reasons described above — parents often attribute this to selfishness. Likewise, when the child calls a strange man "Daddy" or a teacher "Mommy," parents may feel that the child is being disloyal or really doesn't care about them that much. But as we have seen, these behaviors are a consequence, not of bad motives, but of intellectual immaturity.

At the preschool level, then, egocentrism appears in the young child's use of the symbolic function. The child's failure to grasp the difference between transient and abiding representations can be observed in the child's reluctance to share. Likewise the child's failure to discriminate between subjective and objective representations appears in the use of words that he or she has created but that the child assumes that others understand. This type of egocentrism is also reflected in the child's belief that that psychic events like dreams and feelings are tangible things. Finally, the young child's failure to distinguish between the one and the many appears most dramatically in his or her calling strangers "Mommy" or "Daddy."

THE CONCRETE OPERATIONAL PERIOD

From about the age of 6 to about the age of 11, is the time Piaget calls the period of *concrete operations.* These new mental abilities, which constitute a set of internalized actions, permit children to do in their heads what before they had to do with their hands. For example, if a preoperational child is shown two uncut pencils of the same length, placed side by side on a table, and is asked if they are the same length, he or she will agree that this is the case. If one of the pencils is then pushed ahead of the other one, however, the child now will say that one is longer than the other.

One way to solve this problem is to recognize that the action of moving the pencil is reversible. But this requires concrete operations. A behavior that some young children on their way to attaining operations engage in is instructive in this regard. When the two pencils are staggered and the children are asked whether the pencils are the same length, the youngsters try to push the pencils back together so that the ends on both sides are aligned. They are doing with their hands what in a few short months they will be able to do in their heads.

Concrete operations, it should be said, are unconscious; the child does not know that he or she is employing them. In addition, they operate as a set of activities and not as isolated operations. Recall, for example, the preschool child who was having trouble with the one and the many. Concrete operations allow the child to recognize the distinction between a person as an individual and as a member of a class. But this recognition depends on a set of operations, not just one.

To make this point concrete, consider the following problem. In a classroom there are 18 boys and 10 girls. A preoperational child who knows the number of boys and girls is asked whether there are more boys or more children in the room. The preoperational child says that there are more boys than girls and refuses to compare boys with children. He or she does not yet grasp that a child can be both a child and a boy or a girl at the same time. No matter how many times the child is asked about boys and children, the reply is always in terms of boys and girls.

When the same problem is given to a concrete operational child, however, the answer is different. The concrete operational child says that there are more children than boys, because the term, *children,* includes boys as well as girls. Logically we might describe the child reasoning this way, letting C = children, B = boys, and G = girls.

$$G + B = C$$
$$C - B = G$$
$$C - G = B$$
$$C > G$$
$$C > B$$

Once a child says that there are more children than boys, we can infer the other operations about the classes, i.e., that he or she knows that the class of children minus the class of boys equals the class of girls and so on. Concrete operations insure that the child has an organized system of knowledge about the particular subject matter to which he or she has applied them.

Concrete operations make possible many new attainments during the elementary school years. Because they permit syllogistic reasoning, they make it possible for children to learn rules. To be able to learn and to apply rules, one has to be able to move from the general to the particular. In the "spinner" and die-throwing games so popular with early concrete operational children, moving from the general to the particular is required. In spinner games, the rule is that you move your token the number of spaces indicated by the number the arrow of the spinner comes to rest upon. This number varies from trial to trial. To play the game, the child has to move from the general rule to the specific instance, which varies from turn to turn. The same holds true for die-throwing games.

From a logical perspective, this type of rule can be put into syllogism form:

1. Move your token the number of places shown by the spinner arrow.
2. The spinner arrow shows 3.
3. Move your token three places.

This example is not as trivial as it might at first appear. What it illustrates is that in playing games with rules, as in the use of rules generally, a form of concrete operational reasoning is involved. The understanding and following of rules is not just a matter of willfulness and motivation; it is also a matter of intelligence. The preschool child's failure to follow the rules of the game are not due to his or her desire to cheat but rather to the lack of concrete operations that make rule following possible.

The attainment of concrete operations also enables the child to overcome some of the egocentrisms of the preoperational period. Because the child can now grasp the rules of ownership, for example, he or she can distinguish between transient use of a toy and abiding possession. Likewise, concrete operations enable children to distinguish between naming rules and names and to discover that names are ascribed according to naming rules and are not a part of things. This also permits them to distinguish between names that they have created and rule-regulated names. Finally, because they permit children to engage in syllogistic reasoning, concrete operations make it possible for children to distinguish between names used to designate an individual and names used in a generic sense.

If concrete operations free the child from preoperational forms of egocentrism, they nonetheless create new types of egocentrism of their own. The new capacity to form rules brings with it new intellectual problems in distinguishing between transient and abiding rules, between subjective and objective rules, and between the one rule and the many exceptions to that rule. We need to look now at the egocentrism of the concrete operational period.

Let us begin with the problem of distinguishing between transient and abiding rules. Many transient rules are situational. Keeping quiet in a library, for example, is a situational rule that holds for that particular setting. Rules for particular games are transient, as well, because they hold while the game is being played but not when it is not being played. Other rules are not transient place or activity rules but are rather abiding rules. For example, rules about lying and stealing are supposed to transcend particular situations and particular activities.

To truly understand transient and abiding rules, however, requires the mental abilities of the next stage of cognitive development. This is true, because the differentiation between transient and abiding rules requires a kind of propositional logic in which propositions (rules) rather than classes or relations are the elements. Although we talk about the mental operations of adolescence in the next section, the propositional character of understanding transient and abiding rules can be quickly demonstrated.

Suppose we take the rule about silence in the library. To understand its transient character, children need to deal with the following possibilities:

be silent in the library, silent outside	$p \cdot q$
be silent in the library, loud outside	$p \quad \bar{q}$
be loud inside the library, silent outside	$\bar{p} \cdot q$
be loud inside the library, loud outside	$\bar{p} \quad \bar{q}$

These propositions can be combined in many ways, taken 1, 2, 3, or 4 at a time to see their implications. But the point is that once a child is dealing with rules, the logic of concrete operations does not suffice to reason *about* rules; it suffices only to reason *from* rules.

The concrete operational child's failure to distinguish between transient and abiding rules is easy to demonstrate. Rules about lying and stealing are often regarded as transient, situational rules rather than as abiding ones. Children will feel that it is all right to lie in some situations — say, about fighting — but not in others — say, about taking something. The child's shifting sense of what rules are transient and which are abiding often proves frustrating to parents who often say, "I don't know what to believe."

The shift from transient to abiding can occur even with respect to the same rules. Parents are often dismayed that after having reached an agreement about certain rules that they assumed to be abiding (cleaning up rooms, doing the dishes, etc.), children regard them as transient and as open to renegotiation. A similar phenomenon occurs in the classroom when children are allowed to make some of their own rules. Often the teacher, who expected the rules to hold for the semester, finds that they hold only for a few days or weeks.

A child's commitment to rules, then, is handicapped by his or her difficulty in clearly differentiating between rules that are transient and those that are abiding. Like the preschool child who has so much trouble with possession, the school-age child is continually treating transient rules as abiding and abiding rules as transient. His or her discomfiture when challenged in these matters is often misinterpreted by adults as reflecting a guilty conscience rather than as what it really is — namely, intellectual confusion.

The school-age child's failure to differentiate between transient and abiding rules is parallel to his or her inability, frequently, to distinguish between rules that the young person has created and those that are social in origin. In this regard, the school-age child behaves with respect to rules he or she has created much as the preschool child does with respect to self-constructed words. In both cases the mental constructions are externalized and are seen as existing independently of the child and of his or her mental activity.

Before describing some experimental examples, a few anecdotal illustrations may help to give the flavor of this level of egocentrism. Not long ago, an 8-year-old of my acquantance complained that someone had stolen his toothbrush. It turned out that his mother had cleaned the bathroom and put the toothbrush in the holder where it belonged, but where it seldom ended up. When the lad failed to find the toothbrush in its usual place — on the counter — he formed a hypothesis to account for the disappearance. The hypothesis, that the toothbrush was stolen, was immediately externalized and accepted as fact. The corollary of course was that if the toothbrush was stolen, it was unnecessary to look for it.

Such assumptions, or hypotheses, fit within the pattern of syllogistic reasoning characteristic of this age period. The reasoning in this illustration went something like this:

A Toothbrush not in its usual place.

B Toothbrush removed by party or parties unknown.

∴ Unnecessary to look further for toothbrush.

In this instance, the hypothesis is inserted within a logical argument whose conclusion seems necessary and factual. Evidence that the child sees his or her conclusion as necessary comes from his or her response when shown the toothbrush in its holder: "Whoever stole it must have put it back."

This familiar example of reasoning from false premises often occurs in adolescents and adults as well. Many adults come to conclusions from false premises but assume their conclusion is correct, because their reasoning is correct. The difference between the school-age child and at least some adults is that the adult is capable of grasping the difference between a correct logical argument and an incorrect factual one; the child is not.

In some cases, the child's hypothesis becomes extensively elaborated and is believed, not because it is logically necessary but rather because it seems so interesting that one would like it to be true. It is this sort of thinking that gives rise to gossip and

rumor. Some children are better at this sort of construction than others, but most children engage in
it. For example, I once caught a couple of 10-year-
olds skulking about, watching the man next door.
They were sure he was a spy. And a schoolteacher I
knew almost gave up her job, because of the elaborate fantasy two of her students concocted about
her and a male faculty member.

In children's fiction, the tendency of school-age
children to confuse fact with the hypotheses they
have constructed is well illustrated by Penrod
Schofield (Tarkington, 1914/1942). Here is a story
Penrod spins out of whole cloth for his teacher in
order to explain his accidental rudeness to her in a
class as a result of suddenly being awakened from
his daydreams:

> "I want an answer. Why did you shout those
> words at me?"
> "Well," he murmured, "I was just — thinking."
> "Thinking what?" she asked sharply.
> "I don't know."
> "That won't do!"
> He took his left ankle in his right hand and regard-
> ed it helplessly.
> "That won't do, Penrod Schofield," she repeated
> severely. "If that is all the excuse you have to offer I
> shall report your case this instant!"
> And she rose with fatal intent.
> But Penrod was one of those whom the precipice
> inspires. "Well, I *have* got an excuse."
> "Well — she paused impatiently — "what is it?"

He had not an idea, but he felt one coming, and replied automatically, in a plaintive tone:

"I guess anybody that had been through what *I* had to go through, last night, would think they had an excuse."

Miss Spence resumed her seat, though with the air of being ready to leap from it instantly.

"What has last night to do with your insolence to me this morning?"

"Well, I guess you'd see," he returned, emphasizing the plaintive note, "if you knew what *I* know."

"Now, Penrod," she said, in a kinder voice, "I have a high regard for your mother and father, and it would hurt me to distress them, but you must either tell me what was the matter with you or I'll have to take you to Mrs. Houston."

"Well, ain't I going to?" he cried, spurred by the dread name. "It's because I didn't sleep last night."

"Were you ill?" The question was put with some dryness.

He felt the dryness. "No'm; *I* wasn't."

"Then if someone in your family was so ill that even you were kept up all night, how does it happen they let you come to school this morning?"

"It wasn't illness," he returned, shaking his head mournfully. "It was lots worse'n anybody's being sick. It was — it was — well, it was jest awful."

"*What* was?" He remarked with anxiety the incredulity in her tone.

"It was about Aunt Clara," he said.

"Your Aunt Clara!" she repeated. "Do you mean your mother's sister who married Mr. Farry of Dayton, Illinois?"

"Yes — Uncle John," returned Penrod sorrowfully. "The trouble was about him."

. . .

"Yes'm. It all commenced from the first day he let those travelling men coax him into the saloon." Penrod narrated the downfall of his Uncle John at length. In detail he was nothing short of plethoric; and incident followed incident, sketched with such vividness, such abundance of colour, and such verisimilitude to a drunkard's life as a drunkard's life should be, that had Miss Spence possessed the rather chilling attributes of William J. Burns himself, the last trace of skepticism must have vanished from her mind. Besides, there are two things that will be believed of any man whatsoever, and one of them is that he has taken to drink. And in every sense it was a moving picture which, with simple but eloquent words, the virtuous Penrod set before his teacher.

His eloquence increased with what it fed on; and as with the eloquence so with self-reproach in the gentle bosom of the teacher. She cleared her throat with difficulty once or twice, during his description of his ministering night with Aunt Clara. "And I said to her," 'Why, Aunt Clara, what's the use of takin' on so about it?' And I said, 'Now, Aunt Clara, all the crying in the world can't make things any better.' And then she'd just keep catchin' hold of me, and sob and kind of holler, and I'd say, *'Don't* cry, Aunt Clara — *please* don't cry.'"

Then, under the influence of some fragmentary survivals of the respectable portion of his Sunday adventures, his theme became more exalted; and, only partially misquoting a phrase from a psalm, he related

how he had made it of comfort to Aunt Clara, and
how he had besought her to seek Higher guidance in
her trouble.

The surprising thing about a structure such as Penrod was erecting is that the taller it becomes the more
ornamentation it will stand. Gifted boys have this
faculty of building magnificence upon cobwebs —
and Penrod was gifted. Under the spell of his really
great performance, Miss Spence gazed more and more
sweetly upon the prodigy of spiritual beauty and
goodness before her, until at last, when Penrod came
to the explanation of his "just thinking," she was
forced to turn her head away.

"You mean, dear," she said gently, "that you were
all worn out and hardly knew what you were saying?"

"Yes'm."

"And you were thinking about all those dreadful
things so hard that you forgot where you were?"

"I was thinking," he said simply, "how to save
Uncle John."

And the end of it for this mighty boy was that the
teacher kissed him [pp. 64–73]!

The tendency of the school child to mistake his
or her hypotheses for reality has been demonstrated
experimentally as well. In one study (Weir, 1964)
children from 5 to 18 years of age were tested on a
probability learning task. The subjects were confronted with a box that had three knobs and a pay-
off chute. Each subject participated individually
and was told to press the knobs in such a way as to
make the machine pay off as frequently as possible.
The young children were "paid off" in M & M's,
which dropped into the chute when the "right"

knobs were pressed; the older children and adolescents were paid off in tokens that could be turned in for a variety of rewards appropriate to their age level.

Unbeknownst to the participants, the knobs were preprogrammed in the following way. One of the knobs paid off 66 out of 100 presses, in a random sequence. Another of the knobs paid off 33% of the time, again in a random sequence. The remaining knob did not pay off at all. Accordingly, the correct solution to the problem was to press the 66% knob all of the time. To arrive at this solution, the subject had to estimate, on the basis of experience, the probability of any one button paying off per number of times pressed.

The results were interesting. The preoperational children (5–7) assumed that one or another of the knobs would pay off the most, and they quickly learned to push only the 66% knob. Adolescents (12–18), on the other hand, assumed that it was some pattern of knobs that had to be pushed; and they tried out elaborate arrangements such as 1, 22, 333, 11; 22, 33, 1; 22, 3, and so on. Eventually, as a result of these explorations, they discovered that one knob always paid off more than the others, and they settled upon pushing this knob only.

The concrete operational children (8–11) had much more difficulty, and some of them seemed unable to solve the problem. What happened was that the school-age children started, like the adolescents, with an assumption that the solution to the problem involved finding a pattern of knob pressing and not a single most productive knob. However, unlike the adolescents, they were unwilling to give up this assumption. Indeed, rather than trying out a number of hypotheses, they stuck with one, which was: "If you win, you stick with the knob; but if you lose, you shift to another." The concrete operational children seemed reluctant to give up this strategy; and when it didn't work, they blamed the machine!

In this instance, the children clearly mistook a subjective rule — one that they had formulated — for an objective one — the one that actually operated in this situation. Elsewhere (Elkind, 1973), I have called such confusions between subjective and objective rules *assumptive realities.* Whenever a person assumes that a rule or hypothesis is necessarily correct and tries to make the facts fit the hypothesis, we have an instance of an assumptive reality. In the example given earlier, to illustrate, the child operating on the assumption that his toothbrush had been stolen was reacting to an assumptive reality.

Another study (Peel, 1960) provides still additional evidence of how concrete operational children confuse objective and subjectively derived hypotheses and how they operate under assumptive realities. In this study, 9- and 14-year-old students in England were read a passage about Stonehenge, a structure on Salisbury Plain in Wiltshire, England, where huge stones have been erected in a complex pattern. In the passage, the arrangement of the stones was described in detail, and the subjects were asked whether the stones had been placed there as a fort or as a religious shrine. After they gave their answers and their reasons, they were given additional facts that went against their conclusion. If they said it was a fort, they were given facts that supported its being a shrine; and if they said it was a shrine, they were given facts to buttress the opinion that it was a fort.

The results were straightforward. In arriving at their decision, the adolescents made use of a number of facts that had been provided in the paragraph. In supporting their opinions, they listed the facts that favored it. When the adolescents were given additional facts that seemed to contradict their original decision, they appeared to weigh both sets of facts. If they felt that the new evidence outweighed the old evidence they had been given, they changed their decision from fort to shrine or vice versa. They seemed to recognize that their initial choice was a hypothesis, not a fact.

The performance of the 9-year-olds was quite different. In making their decision as to whether the stones were a fort or a shrine, they seemed to look for one, or at most two, strong facts. Even more interesting was their response to the presentation of new facts contrary to the conclusion they had reached. What the 9-year-olds did when confronted with the new evidence was to rationalize it so as to make it support their original hypothesis or assumptive reality. In effect, they wanted to make the facts fit the hypothesis rather than to change the hypothesis to fit the facts.

It should be said that the tendency to operate upon assumptive realities, to confuse subjective rules with objective ones, is not unique to childhood. All of us operate upon such assumptions some of the time. Interpersonal relations are clogged with such assumptions. All it takes, for example, is for someone to be late for a meeting or a date. Often we make assumptions about the reasons for the delay that we are reluctant to give up, despite the late comer's protestations or "excuses." Any explanation that does not correspond with our own prejudgment is, of necessity, an excuse.

As I have said earlier, the difference between children and adults in these regards is a matter of mental ability. Most adults have the capacity to check a hypothesis against the facts and to accept or reject the hypothesis accordingly. When we fail to do this, it is usually for affective, rather than for cognitive, reasons. An investigator who clings to a cherished hypothesis despite much data to the contrary is a case in point. Though such tenacity may on occasion be appropriate, more often it results in a sad waste of human energy and ability.

In the case of children, the tendency to operate upon assumptive realities is largely the result of intellectual immaturity. At this stage, children do not yet have the mental operations that make possible holding one variable constant while changing another. It is the ability to deal with multiple variable situations that enables adolescents and adults to grasp the difference between their subjective constructions and those that are in accord with objective reality.

At the concrete operational level, children also fail to differentiate between rules and exceptions to rules — between, if you will, rules for the one and rules for the many. In this regard children are more advanced linguistically than they are cognitively. Carol Chomsky (1969) has demonstrated that during the concrete operational period, children begin to be aware of the exceptions to grammatical rules. They begin to recognize, for example, that the plural *s* is not always necessary, that some verb forms are irregular, and so on.

But learning that there are exceptions to rules in other instances is more difficult. For example, in Kohlberg's (1972) scheme of moral development, the morality of individual conscience as against obedience to authority is not usually observed until adolescence. The Stage 3 and 4 levels of morality characteristic of the concrete operational period are described as follows:

> Stage 3. Good-boy-good-girl orientation. Good behavior is that which pleases others and is approved by them. There is much conformity to stereotypical images of what is "natural" behavior. (Kohlberg, 1972, p. 160)
>
> Stage 4. Orientation toward authority, fixed rules and the maintenance of the social order. Right behavior consists of doing one's duty, showing respect for authority and maintaining the social order for its own sake." (Kohlberg, 1972, p. 160)

In contrast, the morality of Stages 5 and 6 is described as the morality of self-accepted principles and standards.

In effect, therefore, the concrete operational child does not recognize that rules and laws are subject to many interpretations and that the individual is often responsible for interpreting the law in specific instances. Children want rules to be enforced without regard to particular circumstances. Indeed, they often interpret the adults' adaptation of rules to particular circumstances as a violation of the law.

The concrete operational child's difficulty with rules for the one and rules for the many causes difficulty at home and at school. At school, children are often reluctant to accept concessions to rules made on the basis of illness, handicaps, or whatever. The usual response is that "if I have to do it, he or she should have to do it." Rules should hold for everyone equally regardless of situation. And in the home, one encounters a similar phenomenon. School-age children are reluctant to have rules bend to circumstances. "When I was his age, I didn't have a bike; so he shouldn't have a bike." Or, "When I was her age, I went to sleep at 9:00; so she should go to sleep then." The anger generated by such "deviations" is fueled by the belief that rules reflect external authority and are not susceptible to individual interpretation.

On the other hand, the understanding that rules have to be interpreted to fit particular circumstances is generally understood at adolescence. In a family of my acquaintance, there are three daughters, all now in their teens. The oldest, who is 17, has never been permitted to date alone, because her eagerness to please boys might be taken advantage of. Her younger sister is quite different in this respect and is the type not to be taken advantage of. The older daughter recognized this and urged her mother to let the younger daughter single date, even though she herself was not permitted to do so. This reflects the morality of individual responsibility and circumstance that is seldom seen in childhood.

Before closing this section, the self-concept elaborated at this stage should be remarked upon. At this stage the child begins to think of himself or herself as a lawful being, as a rule maker, a rule follower, and a rule breaker. A healthy self-concept involves all three components in roughly equal measure. But some children begin to see themselves primarily as rule breakers and become behavior problems. Others see themselves primarily as rule followers and become conformists. Those who see themselves as primarily rule makers often become leaders.

The concrete operational period is, then, one in which hypotheses and rule making are very prominent. Egocentrism occurs when children fail to differentiate between transient and abiding rules, between rules and hypotheses that are subjective and those that are objective, and between rules that hold for the many and rules that hold for the one. The egocentrism of this period results in conflicts at home and at school that are characteristic of this age period but that must be attributed to intellectual immaturity rather than to bad motives.

THE FORMAL OPERATIONAL PERIOD

At about the age of 11 to 12, most young people begin to develop a new set of mental abilities that Piaget terms "formal operations." These new operations are "formal" in the sense that they permit young people to operate upon, or think about, concrete operations. Formal operations are thus second-order operations that permit the manipulation of first-order operations. In a sense, formal operations are to concrete operations what algebra is to arithmetic. Indeed, one reason algebra is not taught until adolescence is that is requires formal operations.

Before describing the consequence of formal operations, their functioning should be described in a little more detail. In the algebraic formula $(a + b) (a + b) = a^2 + 2ab + b^2$ the letters can stand for any numbers whatsoever. The algebraic statement is purely formal in the sense that it merely says that there are two ways of expressing the same operations. That is to say, the algebraic equation is really a statement about the equality of operations rather than about the equality of numbers. Children can understand this equality concretely, with respect to specific numbers (e.g., that $[4 + 3] [4 + 3] = 49$), but not in the formal or algebraic sense given above.

In the same way, formal operations also make possible the understanding of logic on a formal basis. The adolescent grasps the formal statement that if all A are B and all B are C, then all A are C regardless of what the letters represent. Likewise, the adolescent with formal operations can also deal with propositional logic or truth functional logic. Truth functional logic permits the testing of hypotheses on a purely formal basis; it makes possible the kind of thinking required in scientific experimentation. Consider the following statements:

It is raining and cold.	p	q
It is raining and not cold.	p	$\bar{q}$
It is not raining and cold.	$\bar{p}$	q
It is not raining and not cold.	$\bar{p}$	$\bar{q}$

Now regardless of the actual weather outside, these statements can be combined in various ways in order to look at their possible relationships. For example, the combination of $\bar{p}\ q \lor p\ \bar{q}$ would suggest that rain and cold are mutually exclusive or *disjunctive*. On the other hand, the combination $p\ q \lor \bar{p}\ q \lor \bar{p}\ q \lor \bar{p}\ \bar{q}$ would suggest that rain and cold are *independent*. In fact, the four propositions can be combined in 16 different ways (taken, 0, 1, 2, 3, and 4 at a time) to yield 16 possible formal relationships between propositions. These can then be used to test empirical happenings, but the combinations themselves are not empirical; they are formal.

The capacity to engage in formal operational thinking makes possible a whole new level of comprehension for adolescents, and it enables them to overcome the egocentrism of the concrete operational period. The rules that the concrete operational child has trouble with can be treated formally by adolescents. By dealing with rules as propositions that can be combined in various ways, adolescents can distinguish between those that are transient and those that are abiding, between subjective and objective rules, and between rules that hold for the one and rules that hold for the many.

Formal operations have other benefits as well. They permit adolescents to grasp metaphor and simile, to fully comprehend historical time and geographical space, to construct ideals, and to grasp contrary-to-fact conditions. In addition, formal operational thinking also enables young people to conceptualize and to think about their own thinking. Adolescents become reflective and contemplative. It is a period during which they develop a *reflective self*, an awareness of the self as a thinker.

Although formal operations greatly expand the adolescent's intellectual capacity and allow him or her to overcome the egocentrisms of childhood, they nonetheless give rise to egocentrisms of their own. In the case of adolescents, however, egocentrism has a different origin than it does at earlier stages. The egocentrism of adolescence involves lack of differentiation as does all egocentrism, but the cause is not lack of intellectual power. Rather, what young adolescents lack is experience; and it is the lack of experience, rather than the lack of the necessary intellectual abilities, that accounts for the egocentrism of this age period.

Basically, the egocentrism of the adolescent period centers about thought and thinking. For the first time, the adolescent can think about his or her own thinking and about the thinking of others. But the adolescent's lack of experience in reflective thinking leads him or her into some characteristic egocentric errors that are chronicled below. Again these are failures of differentiation that will be corrected by successive experiences, not by the attainment of new, higher order mental abilities.

First, with respect to transient and abiding thoughts, some well-documented phenomena reflect the adolescent's difficulty in this regard. One well-known phenomenon is that children of adopted parents often make a great effort during adolescence to find their real parents. This search has many dynamic components, but it has intellectual components as well. For example, the understanding of biological inheritance, made possible by formal operations, heightens the young person's curiosity about his or her biological parents. But it also makes the biological parents' emotional commitment appear to be abiding and the adoptive parents' emotional commitment to be more transient. Once young people can conceive of their biological lineage, they sometimes fail to differentiate between biological and psychological parentage and assume that the biological parents' emotional commitment must be abiding whereas the adoptive parents' commitment must be transient. Fortunately, most adoptive young people come through this period to a fuller appreciation of the commitment of their adoptive parents.

The failure to distinguish between transient and abiding thoughts shows itself in other less dramatic ways. A young person who is embarrassed among friends or acquaintances will be heard to say, "I can't see them ever again, my life is destroyed." The young person assumes that a momentary embarrassment will live permanently in other people's consciousness. It seems abiding to the young person but is usually transient to everybody else. I have called such embarrassing experiences that live on in a person's memory long after the event *abiding moments*. When the adolescent meets the same people again in other circumstances, he or she is sure that the experience is as vivid in their memory as it is in his or her own. Usually, this is far from being the case.

If we turn now to the differentation between the objective and the subjective, we encounter still another well-known phenomenon of early adolescence — namely, self-consciousness. Young adolescents are unusually aware of the people around them. When these people are adults, the young adolescent — depending on his or her personality — may appear excessively shy or expressively extroverted. When adult males are around, for example, young adolescent girls often appear flustered and shyly flirtatious. With younger siblings, however, the self-consciousness often takes an abrasive form, and unexpecting siblings often get berated for spying and not minding their own business.

The self-consciousness of the young adolescent can be demonstrated experimentally as well. In one study (Elkind & Bowen, in press), 4th-, 6th-, 8th-, and 12th-grade students responded to a set of items dealing with exposing themselves to an audience either under embarrassing or self-revealing circumstances. Results showed that there was a regular increase with age in reluctance to reveal oneself to an audience until grade 8. By grade 12, this reluctance had declined considerably. In short, the 13- and 14-year-olds were the most reluctant of all of the age groups tested to reveal themselves to the audience.

I have suggested that the self-consciousness of the young adolescent derives from the failure to differentiate between the objective and the subjective in the realm of thought. What happens, I believe, is this. Thanks to formal operations, young people can now think about other people's thinking. But they do not differentiate between their personal concerns and preoccupations and those of other people. Because their bodies and minds have undergone a dramatic change in a brief time, they are obsessed with their own bodies and minds. And because they cannot yet differentiate between the subjective content of their own thoughts and the objective content of the thoughts of others, they assume that others are as interested and observant of them as they are of themselves. Hence the self-consciousness of early adolescence.

appeased when they imagine the anger of the adults who witness the damage in the morning.

It should be said that the imaginary audience, like many other egocentric constructions, does not disappear entirely as young people gain in experience and sophistication. Even as adults, many of us occasionally behave in response to an imaginary audience. This is particularly true when we are in strange places. It also happens when we are doing something we feel is wrong. The couple having an affair, each married to different partners, is sure that everyone they meet in the hotel or restaurant is privy to their secret. When people are under the influence of strong emotion, the differentiation between subjective concerns and the concerns of others often breaks down.

The last failure of differentation at the level of thought has to do with the one and the many, with the universal and the particular. As in the failure to differentiate between subjective and objective concerns, the failure to differentiate between ideas that are unique and ideas that are universal results in a particular construction. If — thanks to the imaginary audience — everyone is watching you and thinking about you, it must be the case that you are special and unique. To the young adolescent, who is experiencing many feelings and ideas for the first time, it is as if he or she were the first person on earth to experience these feelings. This belief in the uniqueness of one's feelings, thoughts, and experiences is what I have called (Elkind, 1967) the *personal fable*; it is a story that one tells oneself but that is not true.

The personal fable, like the imaginary audience, is a motivational construction. Before turning to its effects, however, it is necessary to show how it reflects a failure to differentiate between the unique and the universal. A young woman who falls in love for the first time is enraptured with the experience, which is entirely new and thrilling. But she fails to differentiate between what is new and thrilling to herself and what is new and thrilling to humankind. It is not surprising, therefore, that this young lady says to her mother, "But mother, you don't know how it feels to be in love." And it is in the context of the personal fable that one has to interpret the remark of a young man who said, "Dad, nobody in the whole world wants a car as badly as I do."

It is easy to observe the other side of the fable as well, the belief that what is unique to the individual is common to everyone. A young woman, for example, has a slight blemish on her cheek. She regards it as ugly and believes that she is ugly and is convinced that everyone else shares her opinion. In this instance she has taken a personal evaluation, which could well be unique to her, and assumed that it is common to everyone. Consequently, she feels badly about herself. On a practical note, it does not help a young person to argue with his or her personal fable. Rather, a better strategy is to accept the fable but help him or her to look at experiences that would modify it. For the girl with the blemish, it is more helpful to say, "Well, you may be right about the blemish; what do people say or do about it that makes you feel this way?" than to say, "That's nonsense — you are a beautiful girl."

As a motivational force, the personal fable can have positive consequences. The young person who feels that he or she is unique may strive to excel in music, literature, sports, or other areas of endeavor. The sense of "specialness" can also be a source of personal strength and comfort in the face of the many, inevitable social, academic, and familial trials and tribulations of adolescence. In the end, the personal fable, as all fables, has a moral that *is* true — namely, that an individual person has value and worth.

But if the personal fable has positive motivational consequences, it has negative ones as well. The sense of uniqueness may give rise to recklessness if it is thought of as "others will get hurt and die but not me." Young men who play "chicken" in cars may think this way. Likewise, young people may experiment with drugs under the mistaken belief that "other people will get hooked, but not me." And many young women get pregnant, even though they know about birth control, at least in part because they are convinced that conception will never happen to them. Clearly, in each case the personal fable combines with other motives to produce the resulting behavior; it is not the sole cause. But in dealing with such young people, one needs to take account of the personal fable as well as of the other dynamics.

As in the case of the imaginary audience, the personal fable does not entirely disappear as we grow older. The belief that we are special, that others will grow old and die but not us, is a necessary and adaptive conception. The notion that we have special worth and importance is a healthy defense against the inevitable emotional and physical disappointments of life. It is only when adults, like young adolescents, take the fable too seriously that it becomes maladaptive and loses its real value.

The development of egocentrism, then, gives still additional support to the three themes proposed in these lectures. It is clear, for example, that assumptive realities, the imaginary audience, and the personal fable are constructions that are neither innate (because they change) nor simply learned (inasmuch as they are in opposition to, rather than in conformance with, experience). Secondly, as I tried to make clear in the discussion of agewise changes in egocentrism, the process of construction is continuous; and the very mental operations that free the young person from one level of egocentrism thrust him or her into new, higher level forms of egocentrism. And finally, the egocentric constructions at each level, though they presuppose both experience and cognitive operations, are genuine creations that cannot be reduced to either one.

Conclusion

In these lectures I have tried to give evidence from different domains and with the aid of different methods for a single contention — namely, that the child's reality is different than the adult's. It might be thought that it was hardly necessary to amass all this material to make such a point, which, after all, is not that revolutionary. And yet, though we may accept in a general way the fact that the child's reality is different than our own, it is a difficult one to maintain in practice. Parents, teachers, and, yes, a good many researchers in child development deal with children as if they and the children shared a common physical and social reality.

So I believe it was necessary to be inclusive regarding the child's reality, because of what might be called adult egocentrism. This egocentrism consists in the belief that children are most like us in their thoughts and least like us in their feelings. In fact, just the reverse is true, and children are most like us in their feelings and least like us in their thoughts. It is because of this egocentrism that adults are simply less polite, rather than less abstract, in their communications with children. And yet children need to hear "please" and "thank you" addressed to them, perhaps more than adults do.

It is difficult to overcome our adult egocentrism with respect to children. It pops up all of the time. A parent fails to keep a promise but doesn't bother to apologize. Or a teacher puts a child's drawing up on the wall without bothering to ask permission. Little hurts, to be sure, but they add up and are perpetuated when the children grow up and become adults themselves. Only as we begin to treat children as like us in their feelings, but different from us in their conception of reality, can we begin to break the chains of misunderstanding that leave us all a little less human than we might otherwise be.

References

Allport, G. *The individual and his religion.* New York: MacMillan, 1953.

Bovet, P. *The child's religion.* New York: Dutton, 1928.

Briggs, C. H., & Elkind, D. Cognitive development in early readers. *Developmental Psychology,* 1973, *9,* 279–280.

Briggs, C. H., & Elkind, D. Characteristics of early readers. *Perceptual and Motor Skills,* 1977, *44,* 1231–1237.

Bruner, J. The course of cognitive growth. *American Psychologist,* 1964, *19,* 1–15.

Chomsky, C. S. *The acquisition of syntax in children from 5 to 10.* Cambridge, Mass.: MIT Press, 1969.

Dewey, J. *The child and the curriculum.* Chicago: University of Chicago Press, 1902.

Downing, J. Messing about with the alphabet. *Where,* January 1971, *53,* 13–16.

Elkind, D. The child's conception of his religious denomination I: The Jewish child. *Journal of Genetic Psychology,* 1961, *99,* 209–225.

Elkind, D. The child's conception of his religious denomination II: The Catholic child. *Journal of Genetic Psychology,* 1962, *101,* 185–195.

Elkind, D. The child's conception of his religious denomination III: The Protestant child. *Journal of Genetic Psychology,* 1963, *103,* 291–304.

Elkind, D. Ambiguous pictures for the study of perceptual development and learning. *Child Development,* 1964, *35,* 1391–1396.

Elkind, D. The development of religious understanding in children and adolescents. In M. P. Strommen (Ed.), *Research on religious development.* New York: Hawthorne, 1971.

Elkind, D. Cognitive structure in latency behavior. In J. C. Westman (Ed.), *Individual differences in children.* New York: Wiley, 1973.

Elkind, D. Perceptual development in children. *American Scientist,* 1975, *63*(5), 535–541.

Elkind, D. *Child development and education: A Piagetian perspective.* New York: Oxford, 1976.

Elkind, D., Anagnostopoulou, I., & Malone, S. Determinants of part–whole perception. *Child Development,* 1970, *41,* 391–397.

Elkind, D. & Bowen, R. Imaginary audience behavior in children and adolescents. *Developmental Psychology.* In press.

Elkind, D., & Deblinger, J. Perceptual training and reading achievement in disadvantaged children. *Child Development,* 1969, *40,* 11–19.

Elkind, D., Horn, J., & Schneider, G. Modified word recognition, reading achievement and perceptual decentration. *Journal of Genetic Psychology,* 1965, *107,* 235–251.

Elkind, D., Koegler, R. R., & Go, E. Effects of perceptual training at three age levels. *Science,* 1962, *137,* 755–756.

Elkind, D., Larson, M. E., & Van Doorninck, W. Perceptual learning and performance in slow and average readers. *Journal of Educational Psychology,* 1965, *56,* 50–56.

Elkind, D., & Scott, L. Studies in perceptual development I: The decentering of perception. *Child Development,* 1962, *33,* 619–630.

Elkind, D., & Weiss, J. Studies in perceptual development III: Perceptual exploration. *Child Development,* 1967, *38,* 1153–1161.

Farkas, M., & Elkind, D. Effects of distance and stimulus position on perceptual comparison at five age levels. *Child Development,* 1974, *45,* 184–188.

Hall, G. S. *Adolescence II.* New York: Appleton–Century–Crofts, 1908.

Heiler, F. *Prayer: A study in the history and psychology of religion.* London: Oxford University Press, 1932.

Hodge, A. *Prayer and its psychology.* New York: Macmillan, 1931.

James, W. *The varieties of religious experience.* New York: Longmans, 1902.

Kohlberg, L. The adolescent as a philosopher: The discovery of the self in a postconventional world. In J. Kagan & R. Coles (Eds.), *Twelve to sixteen: Early adolescence.* New York: W. W. Norton, 1972.

Kohler, W., & Wallach, H. Figural aftereffects. *Proceedings of American Philosophical Society,* 1944, *88,* 269–357.

Kugelmass, S., & Lieblich, A. Perceptual exploration in Israeli children. *Child Development,* 1970, *41,* 1125–1132.

Long, D., Elkind, D., & Spilka, B. The child's conception of prayer. *Journal for the Scientific Study of Religion,* 1967, *vi,* 101–109.

Makita, K. The rarity of reading disability in Japanese children. In S. Chess & A. Thomas (Eds.), *Annual progress in child psychiatry and child development.* New York: Brunner/Mazel, 1969.

Meili–Dworetzki, G. The development of perception in the Rorschach. In B. Klopfer (Ed.), *Developments in the Rorschach technique.* New York: World Book, 1956.

Meyer, J., & Elkind, D. From figurative to operative expectancy in the perceptual judgments of children. *Developmental Psychology,* 1975, 11, *6,* 814–823.

Peel, E. A. *The pupil's thinking.* London: Oldhourne, 1960.

Piaget, J. *The child's conception of the world.* Totowa, N.J.: Littlefield, Adams & Co., 1963. (First English translation, Kegan Paul, 1929).

Piaget, J. *The psychology of intelligence.* London: Routledge & Kegan Paul, 1950.

Piaget, J. *The mechanisms of perception.* New York: Basic Books, 1969.

Reik, T. From spell to prayer. *Psychoanalysis,* 1955, *3,* 3–26.

Starbuck, W. D. *The psychology of religion.* New York: Scribner, 1900.

Tarkington, B. *Penrod.* New York: Doubleday, 1914/1942.

Weir, M. W. Developmental changes in problem solving strategies. *Psychological Review,* 1964, *71,* 473–490.

Werner, H. *Comparative psychology of mental development.* Chicago: Follet, 1948.

Whiteside, J. D., Elkind, D., & Golbeck, S. Effects of exposure duration on part–whole perception in children. *Child Development,* 1976, *27*(2), 498–501.

Winer, B. *Statistical principles in experimental design.* New York: McGraw–Hill, 1962.

Author's Publications

1. (with Seward, J. P., & Shea, R. A.), Evidence for the interaction of drive and reward. *American Journal of Psychology*, 1958, *71*, 404–407.
2. The Syntax of Human Development. Review of Jean Piaget's Logic and Psychology. *Contemporary Psychology*, 1958, *3*, 244.
3. Weight, Size, and the King's Crown. *Jack and Jill*, November, 1958, 16–17.
4. The Tallit. *World Over*, October, 1958, 3 & 11.
5. Death in children's fiction. *Junior Reviewers*, March–April, 1959, p. 3.
6. On doctoral dissertations. *American Psychologist*, 1959, *14*, 695.
7. Why children want stories retold. *Junior Reviewers*, January–February, 1960, p. 11.
8. Interviewing children in a school setting. *Journal of Psychology*, 1960, *50*, 111–117.
9. The development of quantitative thinking. *Journal of Genetic Psychology*, 1961, *98*, 37–46.
10. Children's discovery of the conservation of mass, weight, and volume. *Journal of Genetic Psychology*, 1961, *98*, 219–227.
11. Quantity conceptions in junior and senior high school students. *Child Development*, 1961, *32*, 551–560.
12. The development of the additive composition of

classes in the child. *Journal of Genetic Psychology*, 1961, *99*, 51–57.

13. The child's conception of right and left. *Journal of Genetic Psychology*, 1961, *99*, 269–276.

14. The child's conception of his religious denomination I: The Jewish child. *Journal of Genetic Psychology*, 1961, *99*, 209–223.

15. The child's conception of his religious denomination. *Acta Psychologica*, 1961, *19*, 347.

16. The child's conception of brother and sister. *Journal of Genetic Psychology*, 1962, *100*, 129–136.

17. Quantity conceptions in college students. *Journal of Social Psychology*, 1962, *57*, 459–465.

18. The child's conception of his religious denomination II: The Catholic child. *Journal of Genetic Psychology*, 1962, *101*, 185–193.

19. (with Elkind, Sally). Varieties of religious experience in young adolescents. *Journal for the Scientific Study of Religion*, 1962, *11*, 102–112.

20. (with Scott, Lee). Studies in perceptual development I: The decentering of perception. *Child Development*, 1962, *33*, 619–630.

21. (with Koegler, R. R., & Go, Elsie). Effects of perceptual training at three age levels. *Science*, 1962, *137*, 3532–7.

22. The child's conception of his religious denomination III: The Protestant child. *Journal of Genetic Psychology*, 1963, *103*, 291–304.

23. On reprint requests. *American Psychologist*, 1963, *18*, 259.

24. (with Koegler, R. R., & Go, Elsie). Field independence and concept formation. *Perception and Motor Skills*, 1963, *17*, 383–386.

25. Discrimination, seriation and numeration of size dif-

ferences in young children. *Journal of Genetic Psychology*, 1964, *104*, 275–296.

26. Ambiguous pictures for the study of perceptual development and learning. *Child Development*, 1964, *35*, 1391–1396.

27. Piaget's semi-clinical interview and the study of spontaneous religion. *Journal for the Scientific Study of Religion*, 1964, *4*, 40–46.

28. Age changes in the meaning of religious identity. *Review of Religious Research*, 1964, *6*, 36–40.

29. L'appartenance religieuse dans la pensee de l'enfant. *Lumen Vitae*, 1964, *19*, 443–456.

30. (with Koegler, R. R., & Go, Elsie). Studies in perceptual development II: Part–whole perception. *Child Development*, 1964, *35*, 81–90.

31. Reading and logic. *Colorado Education Association Journal*, 1965, *80*, 30–31.

32. How children learn to read. *Science*, 1965, *149*, 1395.

33. (with Koegler, R. R., Go, Elsie, & Van Doorninck, W.). Effects of perceptual training on unmatched samples of brain injured and familial retardates. *Journal of Abnormal Psychology*, 1965, *70*, 107–110.

34. (with Horn, J., & Schneider, Gerrie). Modified word recognition, reading achievement and perceptual decentration. *Journal of Genetic Psychology*, 1965, *107*, 235–251.

35. (with Larson, M. E., & Van Doorninck, W.). Perceptual learning and performance in slow and average readers. *Journal of Educational Psychology*, 1965, *56*, 50–56.

36. Conceptual orientation shifts in children and adolescents. *Child Development*, 1966, *37*, 493–498.

37. Conservation across illusory transformations in young children. *Acta Psychologica*, 1966, *25*, 389–400.

38. Non-verbal exercises for remedial reading instruction. *Colorado School Journal*, March 1966, 37–38.

39. (with David, H. P., & Elkind, D.). Family adaptation overseas: Some mental health perspectives. *Mental Hygiene*, 1966, *50*.

40. (with Binnie, C., & Stewart, J.). A comparison of the visual perceptual ability of acoustically impaired and hearing children. *International Audiology*, 1966, *V*, 2, 238–241.

41. The developmental psychology of religion. In A. H. Kid and J. L. Rivoire (Eds.), *Perceptual Development*. New York: International University Press, 1966, 193–225.

42. Middle class delinquency. *Mental Hygiene*, 1967, *51*, 80–84.

43. Egocentrism in adolescence. *Child Development*, 1967, *38*, 1025–1034.

44. Piaget and Montessori. *Harvard Educational Review*, 1967, *37*, 4, *535–545*.

45. Piaget's Theory of Perceptual Development: Its Application to Reading and Special Education. *Journal of Special Education*, 1967, *1*, 4, 357–361.

46. Evolution des conceptions de la priere chez l'enfant. *Lumen Vitae*, 1967, 357–361.

47. (with Long, D., & Spilka, B.). The child's conception of prayer. *Journal of Scientific Study of Religion*, 1967, *VI*, 101–109.

48. (with Van Doorninck, W., & Schwarz, Cynthia). Perceptual activity and concept attainment. *Child Development*, 1967, *38*, 1153–1161.

49. (with Weiss, Jutta). Studies in perceptual development III: Perceptual Exploration. *Child Development*, 1967, *38*, 553–561.

50. Piaget's conservation problems. *Child Development,* 1967, *38,* 15–27.

51. Cognition in infancy and early childhood. In Y. Brack-bill (Ed.), *Handbook of Infancy and Early Childhood,* Wilkins. New York: Free Press, 1967.

52. (Ed.), *Six psychological studies by J. Piaget.* New York: Random House, 1967.

53. Always Changing, Always the Same. *Childhood Education,* 1967–68, 292–300.

54. Cognitive structure and adolescent experience. *Adolescence,* 1967–68, 427–434.

55. Jean Piaget: Giant in the Nursery. *New York Times Magazine,* May 26, 1968.

56. Answer the kid. *New York Times Magazine,* September 28, 1968.

57. (with Barocas, R., & Rosenthal, H.). Combinatorial thinking in adolescents from graded and ungraded classrooms. *Perceptual and Motor Skills,* 1968, *27,* 1015–1018.

58. Cognitive development in adolescence. In J. F. Adams (Ed.), *Contributions to the Understanding of Adolescence.* Boston: Allyn & Bacon, 1968.

59. Preschool Education: Instruction or Enrichment. *Childhood Education,* February, 1969, 321–328.

60. Piagetian and Psychometric approaches to intelligence. *Harvard Educational Review,* 1969, *39,* 319–337.

61. (with Barocas, R., & Johnsen, P.). Concept production in children and adolescents. *Human Development,* 1969, *12,* 10–21.

62. (with Deblinger, JoAnn). Perceptual training and reading achievement in disadvantaged children. *Child Development,* 1969, *40,* 1, 11–19.

63. Conservation and concept formation. In D. Elkind &

J. H. Flavell (Eds.), *Studies in Cognitive Development* (Festschrift in honor of Piaget's 70th birthday). New York: Oxford, 1969, pp. 171–189.

64. Reading, logic and perception: An approach to reading instruction. In J. Hellmuth (Ed.), *Educational Therapy,* V. 2. Washington: Special Child Publications, 1969, pp. 195–208.

65. Developmental studies of figurative perception. In L. P. Lipsitt, H. W. Reese (Eds.), *Advances in Child Development and Behavior.* New York: Academic Press, 1969, 4, 2–28.

66. Research and Evaluation in Religious Education. In J. M. Lee & P. C. Rooney (Eds.), *Toward a future for religious education.* Dayton, Ohio: Pflaum Press, 1970, pp. 208–232.

67. A researcher looks at children. In Mary Duckert (Ed.), *Christian Faith and Action in Grades 1–6.* Philadelphia: Westminister Press, 1969, pp. 21–65.

68. The Adolescent. In J. Simpson (Ed.), *Parish Planning for Grades 7–10.* Philadelphia: Westminister Press, 1969, pp. 101–140.

69. (with Flavell, J. H.). (Eds.), *Studies in cognitive development: Essays in honor of Jean Piaget.* New York: Oxford University Press, 1969.

70. Cognitive Development. In L. Lipsitt & H. W. Reese's *Experimental Child Psychology.* New York: Academic Press, 1969.

71. The Case for Preschool Instruction: Fact or Fiction. *Young Children,* January 1970, 132–140.

72. The origins of religion in the child. *Archives de Psychologie* (and in *Review of Religious Research,* 1970, *12,* 1, 35–42).

73. Piaget and Education. Position paper for ERIE and reprinted in *Children and Adolescents,* Oxford University Press, 1970.

74. From Ghetto School to College Campus: Some discontinuities and continuities. Toledo Law Review, 1970 (also in *Journal of School Psychology*, 1971, *9*, 3, 241–245).

75. Erik H. Erikson: Eight Stages of Man. *New York Times Magazine*, April 5, 1970.

76. Of Time and the Child. *New York Times Magazine*, October 11, 1970.

77. Piaget's Educational Philosophy. *Bulletin of the Rochester Mental Health Association*, 1970, *2*, 40–42.

78. Freud, Jung and the Collective Unconscious. *New York Times Magazine*, October 4, 1970.

79. The new first grader. *Elementary Education in the Church*, September–November, 1970, 6–10.

80. Experience and Cognitive Growth. In G. Engstrom (Ed.), *Open Education*, Washington, D.C.: NAEYC, 1970, pp. 10–22.

81. Exploitation and the generational conflict. *Mental Hygiene*, 1970, *54*, 490–497 (Rochester Review, 1969).

82. (with Medvene, L., & Rockway, A. S.). Representational Level and Concept Production in Children and Adolescents. *Developmental Psychology*, *2*, 85–89.

83. (with Anagnostopoulou, Irene, & Malone, Sue). Determinants of Part–Whole Perception. *Child Development*, 1970, *41*, 391–397.

84. (with Deblinger, JoAnn, & Adler, D.). Motivation and Creativity: The Context Effect. *American Educational Research Association Journal*, 1970, *7*, 351–357.

85. On perceptual development. In J. Alken et al. (Eds.), *Language Behavior*. The Hague: Mouton & Co., 1970, pp. 21–33.

86. (with Sameroff, A. Developmental Psychology. In P.

Mussen & M. Rosenzweig (Eds.), *Annual Review of Psychology.* Palo Alto: Annual Reviews, Inc., 1970, pp. 191–238.

87. *Children and Adolescents: Interpretative Essays on Jean Piaget.* New York: Oxford University Press, 1970.

88. Sense and nonsense about preschools. *Parents' Magazine,* March, 1971, 51–54.

89. What preschoolers need most. *Parents' Magazine,* May, 1971.

90. The Psychoanalyst as Revolutionary:Wilhelm Reich. *New York Times Magazine,* April 18, 1971.

91. The continuing influence of Jean Piaget. *Grade Teacher,* May/June, 1971.

92. Teacher Child Contracts. *School Review,* 1971, *79,* 575–589.

93. Increasing and Releasing Human Potentials. *Childhood Education,* April, 1971, pp. 346–348.

94. Early Childhood Education: A Piagetian Perspective. *The Principal,* September, 1971, 48–55.

95. Measuring Young Minds. *Horizon Magazine,* Winter, 1971.

96. Introduction, *Cognitive Studies* II. J. Hellmuth (Ed.), New York: Bruner/Mazel, 1971.

97. Egocentrism in Young Children. *AAUW Journal,* November, 1971.

98. Too Much Matter Over Mind? *Early Years,* December, 1971, p. 22.

99. Understanding the Third Grader. *Elementary Education in the Church,* December, 1971.

100. Praise and Imitation. Essay Review of Robert Coles "Erik Erikson." In *Saturday Review,* January 16, 1971.

101. *What Do You Think?* Film (34-minute 16 mm. sound-color) produced by Geneva Press, Philadelphia, 1971.

102. Review of "Who Shall Live? Medicine, Technology, Ethics" K. Vaux (Ed.), in *Review of Religious Research,* 1971, *12,* 196.

103. Review of Jean Piaget's "The Mechanisms of Perception" in *American Educational Research Journal,* 1971, VIII, 393–396.

104. Two Approaches to Intelligence: Piagetian and Psychometric. In D. R. Green, M. P. Ford and G. Flamer (Eds.) *Measurement and Piaget.* New York: McGraw Hill, 1971, pp. 12–33.

105. Exploitation in Middle Class Delinquency. In V. C. Vaughn (Ed.) *Issues in Human Development.* Washington: U. S. Government Printing Office, 1971, pp. 141–146.

106. The Development of Religious Understanding in Children and Adolescents. In M. S. Strommen (Ed.) *Research on Religious Development.* New York: Hawthorne, pp. 655–685.

107. Children's Thinking Patterns. *Encyclopedia of Education,* New York: MacMillan and Free Press, 1971, 152–156.

108. Introduction to K. Lovell, *An Introduction to Human Development.* Glenview, Illinois: Scott, Foresman and Co., 1971.

109. Introduction to K. O'Connor, *Learning an Introduction.* Glenview, Illinois: Scott, Foresman and Co., 1971.

110. *A Sympathetic Understanding of the Child: Six to Sixteen.* Boston: Allyn and Bacon, 1971.

111. Cognition in Infancy and Early Childhood. In J. Eliot (Ed.) *Human Development and Cognitive Processes.* New York: Holt, 1971, 507–540.

112. (with Schoenfeld, Eva). Identity and Equivalence Conservation at Two Age Levels. *Developmental Psychology,* 1972, *6,* 529–533.

113. (with Weiner, I. B.). *Child Development: A Core Ap-*

proach. New York: John Wiley & Sons, 1972.

114. Review of Psychology and Epistemology by Jean Piaget. Boston: *Sunday Herald Traveler,* January 30, 1972.

115. Demythologizing Freud. Essay reveiw of Henri F. Ellenberger's The Discovery of the Unconscious. *Contemporary Psychology, 17,* 56–59.

116. Cognitive growth cycles in mental development. In D. Katz (Ed.) *Nebraska Symposium on Motivation, 1971.* Lincoln, Nebraska, 1972, 1–31.

117. (with Weiner, I. B.). *Readings in Child Development.* New York: John Wiley & Sons, 1972.

118. 'Good me' or 'Bad me' – The Sullivan Approach to Personality, *New York Times Magazine,* June 18, 1972.

119. Coeducation and sexual development. *Medical Aspects of Human Sexuality.* November, 1972, p. 164.

120. Ethnicity and reading: Three avoidable dangers. In H. Tanyzer & J. Karl (Eds.), *Reading Children's Books and our Pluralistic Society.* Newark, Delaware: IRA, 1972, pp. 4–8.

121. Some misunderstandings about how children learn. *Today's Education,* 1972.

122. Piaget and Science Education. *Science and Children,* November, 1972, pp. 9–12.

123. What does Piaget say to the teacher? *Today's Education,* November, 1972, pp. 47–48.

124. (with Hamsher, J. Herbert). Anatomy of melancholy, *Saturday Review,* September 30, 1972, pp. 54–59.

125. *Piaget in Childhood Education,* Listener In-Service Cassette Library (4 tapes).

126. Academic Excellence: Too much, too soon? *Teacher,* December, 1972, pp. 8–10.

127. Children view politics. Review of "The Child's Construction of Politics" by R. W. Connell, *Contemporary Psychology,* 1972, *17,* pp. 678–679.

128. *The Child's Point of View.* Film Strip Series, Parent Magazine Enterprises.

129. (with Mussen, P., Rosenzweig, M., Aronson, E., Feshbach, S., Geiwitz, P. J., Glickman, S., Murdock, B. & Wertheimer, M.). *Psychology: An Introduction.* Boston: D. C. Heath & Co., 1973. (Section 5, Cognitive and Educational Psychology, pp. 344–345).

130. Cognitive Structure in Latency Behavior. In J. C. Westman (Ed.). *Individual Differences in Children.* New York: John Wiley & Sons, 1973, pp. 105–117.

131. Borderline Retardation in Low and Middle Income Adolescents. In R. M. Allen, A. D. Cortazzo and R. P. Toister (Eds.) *Theories of Cognitive Development.* Coral Gables: University of Miami Press, 1973, pp. 57–86.

132. Contemporary Issues in Early Childhood Education. *Journal of Research and Development in Education,* 1973, *6,* 118–123.

133. Culture, Change and their Effects on Children. *Social Casework,* 1973, *54,* 360–366.

134. Infant Intelligence. *American Journal of Diseases of Children.* 1973, *126,* 8, 143–144. (Also, *The Australian Journal of Mental Retardation,* 1974, *3,* 1, 6–8.)

135. G. Stanley Hall and the Child Study Movement: Today and Yesterday. *Harvard Educational Review,* 1973, *43,* 3, 417–428.

136. Sullivan in the New York Times. *The William Alanson White Institute, VII,* 3, Spring, 1973. (NEWSLETTER)

137. (with Briggs, C.). Cognitive Development in Early Readers. *Developmental Psychology,* 1973, *9,* 2, 279–280.

138. Learning to Read. *The Instructor,* August/September 1973, LXXXIII, 1, 48.

139. Essay Review of Piaget's and Inhelder's "Memory & Intelligence." New York: Behavioral Science Book Service, December 1973.

140. Black English. *The Instructor,* December 1973, LXXXIII, 4, 26.
141. An Introduction to the Ideas of Jean Piaget. In R. I. Evans (Ed.) *Jean Piaget: The Man and his Ideas.* New York: Dutton & Co., 1973.
142. Perceptual Development. *The Instructor.* January 1974, LXXXIII, 5, 38.
143. *A Sympathetic Understanding of the Child: Birth to Sixteen.* Boston: Allyn and Bacon, 1974. (Second Edition)
144. (with Farkas, M.). Effects of Distance and Stimulus Position on Perceptual Comparison at Five Age Levels. *Child Development,* 1974, *45,* 184–188.
145. (with Mussen, P., Rosenzweig, M., Aronson, E., Feshbach, S., Glickman, S., Murdock, B. & Wertheimer, M.). *Concepts in Psychology: Introductory Readings.* Boston: D. C. Heath & Co., 1974, 215–280.
146. *Children and Adolescents.* New York: Oxford University Press, 1974. (Second Edition)
147. Some Reflections upon Infant Stimulation Studies. In L. G. Fein's (Ed.) *International Understanding.* New York: MSS Information Corporation, 1974.
148. (with Hetzel, D.). British Primary Education. *Tape of the Month in Early Childhood,* 1974. Arlington, Virginia: Childhood Resources, Inc.
149 Commentary on "Erotic Feelings in Infants and Young Children" by Harry Bakwin, M.D. *Medical Aspects of Human Sexuality,* 1974, *8,* 10, 212, 215.
150. (with Dick, S., & Brown, K.). Evaluation of World of Inquiry School, 1969–1972. National Science Foundation – Final Report, August 1974, (mimeo University of Rochester)
151. (with Hetzel, D., & Coe, J.). Piaget and British Primary Education, *Educational Psychologist,* 1974, *11,* 1, 1–10.

152. Reply to Drs. Pasamanick and Knoblock re: Infant Intelligence. *American Journal of Diseases of Children,* 1974, *127,* 5, 759–760.

153. Essay Review of Theta Wolff's "Alfred Binet." *American Journal of Diseases of Children,* 1974, *128,* 11 749–751.

154. Early Childhood Education in the Seventies: What Can We Learn from Past Mistakes? *Contemporary Education,* 1974, *XLV,* 4, 254–260.

155. Cognitive Development and Reading. *Proceedings: Claremont Reading Conference,* 1974, 10–20.

156. Erik H. Erikson: Psychosocial Analyst. Monograph Series, *Major Contributors to Modern Psychotherapy.* Nutley, New Jersey: Hoffmann-LaRoche, Inc., 1974, 25 pp.

157. Encountering Erving Goffman. *Human Behavior,* 1975, *4,* 3, 24–30.

158. Child Development and Education. *Canadian Psychological Review,* 1975, *16,* 2, 81–87.

159. Carl Jung. *Comprehensive Textbook of Psychiatry.* Baltimore: Williams & Wilkins, 1975, Vol. 1, 632–636.

160. Wilhelm Reich. *Comprehensive Textbook of Psychiatry.* Baltimore: Williams & Wilkins, 1975, Vol. 1, 650–654.

161. Piaget. *Human Behavior,* 1975, *4,* 8, 24–31.

162. Recent Research on Cognitive Development in Adolescence. In S. Dragastin's (Ed.) *Adolescence in the Life Cycle.* Washington, D.C.: Hemisphere Publishing Corporation, 1975, 49–61.

163. (with Lyke, N.). Early Education and Kindergarten: Cooperation or Competition? *Young Children,* 1975, *XXX,* 6, 393–399.

164. Perceptual Development in Children. *American Scientist,* 1975, *63,* 5, 535–541.

165. *Cognitive Development.* (Module) Homewood, Illinois: Learning Systems Co., 1975. 32 pp.
166. (with Meyer, J. S.). From Figurative to Operative Expectancy in the Perceptual Judgments of Children. *Developmental Psychology,* 1975, *11,* 6, 814–823.
167. We Can Teach Reading Better. *Today's Education,* 1975, *64,* 4, 34–38.
168. Comments on Symposium on "Sexual Idiosyncrasies" by A. Auerback, M.D. *Medical Aspects of Human Sexuality,* 1976, *10,* 2, 99–100.
169. *Audio Colloquies.* Charles Serris, Series Editor. (A Harper & Row Media Program.) An Interview with David Elkind. New York: Harper & Row, Publishers, Inc., 1976.
170. Cognitive Frames and Family Interactions. In V. C. Vaughan (Ed.) *The Family: Can it be saved?* Chicago: Year Book Medical Publishers, 1976, 269–278.
171. Cognitive Development and Psychopathology: Observations on egocentrism and ego defense. In E. Schopler and R. J. Reichler (Eds.) *Psychopathology and Child Development.* New York: Plenum Publishing Corp., 1976, 167–184.
172. Child Development in Educational Settings. *Educational Psychologist,* 1976, *12,* 1, 49–58.
173. (with Whiteside, J., Golbeck, S.). Effects of Exposure Duration on Part–Whole Perception in Children. *Child Development,* 1976, *47,* 2, 498–501.
174. Cognitive Adaptation in Latency: The Construction of Social Reality. *Canadian Psychiatric Association Journal,* 1976, *21,* 4, 186–191.
175. *Child Development and Education: A Piagetian Perspective.* New York: Oxford University Press, 1976.
176. Elkind Updates Piaget. *Day Care and Early Education,* 1976, *4,* 1, 9–10.
177. Curriculum Disabled Children. *New York State As-*

sociation for Supervision and Curriculum Development NEWSLETTER, 1976, 16, 5, 1–2.

178. Conceptualizing Adolescence. (Reviews of Judith E. Gallatin, Adolescence and individuality: A conceptual Approach to adolescent psychology and Rolf E. Muus, Theories of adolescence.) *Contemporary Psychology,* 1976, *21,* 8, 538–539.

179. Two Approaches to Child Development: Piaget and Montessori. *The Psychology of the Twentieth Century.* Zurich, Switzerland: Kindler Verlag, 1976.

180. Essay Review of "Erik Erikson: The Power and Limits of a Vision" by Paul Roazen. *New York Times Book Review Section,* December 19, 1976.

181. (with Mussen, P., Rosenzweig, M., Aronson, E., Feshbach, S., Glickman, S., Murdock, B., & Wertheimer, M.). *Psychology: An Introduction* (Second Edition). Boston: D. C. Heath & Co., 1977.

182. (with Hetzel, D.) *Human Development: Contemporary Perspectives* (Human Reader Series). New York: Harper & Row, 1977.

183. Life and Death: Concepts and Feelings in Children. *Day Care and Early Education,* January/February, 1977.

184. (with Briggs, C.). Characteristics of Early Readers. *Perceptual and Motor Skills,* 1977, *44,* 1231–1237.

185. (with Dabek, R.). Personal Injury and Property Damage in the Moral Judgment of Children. *Child Development,* 1977, *48,* 518–522.

186. Humanizing the Curriculum. *Childhood Education,* 1977, *53,* 179–182.

187. The Early Years: The Vital Years. In S. Cohen and T. J. Cominskey (Eds.) *Child Development: Contemporary Perspectives* (Second Edition). Itasca, Illinois: F. E. Peacock Publishers, Inc., 1977 and in

The Journal of the Canadian Association for Young Children, 1977.

188. Review of "The Visual World of the Child" by E. Vurpillot (trans. by W. E. C. Gillham). *American Scientist,* 1977, *65,* 239.

189. Observing classroom frames. *Instructor Magazine,* September, 1977.

190. What children need most. Interview, *Parents Magazine,* July, 1977.

191. Essay Review of "The Rites of Passage." *Chronicle of Higher Education,* July 18, 1977, *XIV,* 15.

192. Review of "Adolescence" by J. E. Horrocks. *Contemporary Psychology,* 1977.

193. Cognitive Growth in Early Childhood. In D. Blanchard (Ed.) *The Month of the Child.* New York: Pace University Press, 1977, 56–61.

194. Introduction to *The Child's Construction of Knowledge: Piaget for Teaching Children* by S. Foreman and D. Kuschner. New York: Brooks Cole, 1977.

IN PRESS

195. Essay Review of "The Grasp of Consciousness" by Jean Piaget. *American Journal of Diseases of Children.*

196. Understanding the Young Adolescent. *Adolescence.*

197. Piaget and Developmental Psychology in America. *Proceedings of the Fifth Annual Symposium of the Piaget Society.*

198. (with Weiner, I.). *Development of the Child.* New York: John Wiley & Sons, Inc., 1978.

199. The Figurative and the Operative in Piagetian Psychology. In M. H. Bornstein & W. Kessen (Eds.) *Psychological Development from Infancy.* Hillsdale, New Jersey: Lawrence Erlbaum Associates.

200. A Sympathetic understanding of the child. Boston: Allyn & Bacon, 1978 (3rd edition).
201. *The Child and Society: Essays in Applied Child Development.* Oxford University Press.
202. The active classroom and children with special needs. In S. J. Meisels (Ed.) *Open Education and Young Children with Special Needs.* Baltimore: University Park Press.
203. Language arts and the young child. *Language Arts,* 1978, *55,* 2–5.
204. *The Child's reality: Three developmental themes.* Hillsdale, New Jersey, Lawrence Erlbaum Associates.
205. Erikson's view of the human life cycle. *Dialogue.*
206. Descriptive concepts can be explanatory. *The Behavioral and Brain Sciences.*
207. Elkind, D., & Bowen, R. Imaginary audience behavior in children and adolescents. *Developmental Psychology.*

Subject Index

	Page
Abiding moments	121
Adherences	8
Affects associated with prayer	39
Assumptive realities (defined)	111
Centered	48
Conception of prayer	
Stage I	35
Stage II	36–37
Stage III	37–38
Conceptual reality	
Concrete operations	97–117
Conservation concepts	75
Content of prayer	39
Decentered	48
Deferred imitation	92
Disordered array	63. 65
Egocentrism (defined)	85
Expectation	70–75
Fantasy associated with prayer	40
Field effects	48
Figurative expectation	71
Figurative wholes	55
Formal operations	117–128
Imaginary audience	123

153

Institutional religion   3, 4, 5
Lawful self   116
Ordered array   63, 66
Operative expectation   71
Operative wholes   55, 60, 61
Participations   8
Perceptual exploration   62
Picture Integration Test (P.I.T.)   57, 60, 61
Perceptual reality   47
Perceptual regulations   48, 49
Perceptual reorganization   49–55
Perceptual schematization   55–62
Perceptual transport   67–70
Personal fable   126
Personal religion   5
Picture Ambiguity Test (P.A.T.)   52, 53
Picture Exploration Test (P.E.T.)   66
Picture Opposition Test (P.O.T.)   73
Picture Uniformity Test (P.U.T.)   68, 70
Psychoanalysis   2
Preoperational period   92–97
Reading   75–83
Reciprocal transport   67
Reflective self   119
Religious identity   5, 8
Religious identity
    Stage I   9–10
    Stage II   18–22
    Stage III   22–26
Self consciousness   121
Semiclinical interview   6
Sensori-motor period   90, 91
Spontaneous religion   4

Syllogistic reasoning	99
Symbolic function	92
Symbolic self	93
Temporal decentering	72
Truth functional logic	118
Unilateral transport	67
Violation of expectation	. 71